ISAIAH
and the
Prophets

THE RELIGIOUS STUDIES
MONOGRAPH SERIES

ISAIAH
and the
Prophets

Inspired Voices from the Old Testament

Edited with an Introduction by
Monte S. Nyman

Associate Editor
Charles D. Tate

VOLUME TEN
IN THE RELIGIOUS STUDIES MONOGRAPH SERIES

Religious Studies Center
Brigham Young University
Provo, Utah

Library of Congress Catalog Card Number: 84-70369
ISBN 0-88494-522-7

First Printing, 1984

Produced and Distributed by
BOOKCRAFT, INC.
Salt Lake City, Utah

Lithographed in the United States of America
PUBLISHERS PRESS
Salt Lake City, Utah

Contents

Preface

A symposium on "Isaiah and the Prophets" was held at Brigham Young University on March 19 and 20, 1982. This two-day symposium was sponsored by the Religious Studies Center of the university and was coordinated by Dr. Monte S. Nyman. The objective of the symposium was to help members of The Church of Jesus Christ of Latter-day Saints come to a better understanding of the message of the Old Testament prophets and their relevance in these latter days. While this was the objective, it is emphasized that the views expressed in the various papers are not necessarily endorsed by The Church of Jesus Christ of Latter-day Saints or by Brigham Young University; each author takes sole responsibility for the views presented in his paper.

There were some who participated in the symposium whose papers are not included in this work because of personal choice or because their presentations have not been committed to writing.

Introduction:
Search the Prophets

Monte S. Nyman

A symposium on Isaiah and the prophets was a fitting occasion for the year 1982, since the Sunday School Gospel Doctrine classes were studying these ancient prophets that year and the membership of the Church had been excited to a curiosity about the lives and teachings of these great men. These men were great, not only because they were prophets, but also because they served in a unique time and situation. They lived in a time when the gospel in its fulness and the Melchizedek Priesthood had been taken from the children of Israel because "they were a stiffnecked people, quick to do iniquity, and slow to remember the Lord their God" (Mosiah 13:29). Their unique situation was that the law of Moses, which was "a law of performances and of ordinances, a law which they were to observe strictly from day to day, to keep them in remembrance of God and their duty towards him" (Mosiah 13:30), had been added to the gospel. These men demonstrated their greatness by rising above these obstacles and preparing themselves to receive the Melchizedek Priesthood so that they might better serve the people. The Prophet Joseph Smith taught that they all were given this higher priesthood:

> Was the Priesthood of Melchizedek taken away when Moses died? All Priesthood is Melchizedek, but there are different portions or degrees of it. That portion which brought Moses to speak with God face to face was taken away; but that which brought the ministry of angels remained.[1]

Then the Prophet added parenthetically, "All the prophets had the Melchizedek Priesthood and were ordained by God himself."[2] This implies that these men did receive that further portion of the priesthood which enabled them to see God face to face. This is also verified by their own testimonies, as is further confirmed by many of the papers in this volume.

The Prophet Joseph Smith said that these ancient prophets "were ordained by God himself." They were also foreordained. God foreordained these noble and great men to come forth when they did that they might fulfill a specific mission to the peoples of their time. This, of course, is confirmed by the Lord's statement to Jeremiah in the beginning of that choice record: "Before I formed thee in the belly I knew thee; and before thou camest forth out of the womb I sanctified thee, and I ordained thee a prophet unto the nations" (Jeremiah 1:5). This is also suggested in the calls given to other prophets, such as Amos (see Amos 7:14-15) and Ezekiel (see Ezekiel 2:1-3:11). It was undoubtedly true of all the prophets. The statement that God himself ordained these men needs some clarification. Since a priesthood ordination is an earthly ordinance, the Old Testament prophets were undoubtedly also ordained by a mortal representative of God upon the earth. This conclusion is drawn from the fact that Joseph Smith ordained Oliver Cowdery and Oliver ordained Joseph after John the Baptist had conferred the Aaronic Priesthood upon them (Joseph Smith—History 1:68-72). However, before their earthly ordination the ancient prophets were personally selected or designated by God for this sacred privilege of holding the Melchizedek Priesthood, having lived up to their premortal foreordination. Since all who hold the Melchizedek Priesthood at any time are foreordained (see Alma 13:1-5), this observation may not seem too significant; however, when one considers the worthiness of these men to be called despite the stiffnecked condition of the children of Israel at that time, their ordination becomes a great compliment to their dedication.

A symposium on these prophets should be significant for several reasons. First of all, their writings were major sources which Jesus and the Apostles used in teaching the gospel in the meridian of time. There are at least forty-two passages which can assuredly be identified as Isaiah's writings quoted in the New Testament. There are also twenty-seven passages from the prophet Jeremiah which can be positively identified, and there are many other passages from the other prophets likewise quoted. How many more passages were included before the many "plain and precious parts" were taken away (see 1 Nephi 13:26-35) can only be left to speculation, but there obviously were some, as shown by Matthew 27:9 and Helaman 8:18-20.

Another reason for such a symposium is that the Book of Mormon prophets quoted extensively from these Old Testament prophets. At least 425 verses from Isaiah are quoted in the Book of

Mormon, not counting repetitions. At least nine verses from the prophet Micah are quoted by the Savior himself, several more than once. There are only three references to Jeremiah in the Book of Mormon (1 Nephi 5:13; 7:14; Helaman 8:20), but these are all significant in authenticating Jeremiah's works. It should be noted that because many of the Old Testament prophets (including Jeremiah, whose ministry overlapped Lehi's) lived and testified after Lehi left Jerusalem, they were not quoted in the Book of Mormon. There is one exception. Although Malachi lived after Lehi left, the Father commanded Jesus to quote the entire third and fourth chapters of his prophecies as he ministered to the Nephites (see 3 Nephi 24, 25). On the other hand, Nephite prophets quoted many other passages from the plates of brass which restore plain and precious parts that had been lost from the record of the Jews (see 1 Nephi 19:10-17; 22:15-17; Jacob 5; Alma 33:3-11).

A third reason for studying the Old Testament prophets is that their writings are being fulfilled in our day. As the Savior ministered among the Nephites, he made this informative declaration:

> Behold, I say unto you that the law is fulfilled that was given unto Moses.
>
> Behold, I am he that gave the law, and I am he who covenanted with my people Israel; therefore, the law in me is fulfilled, for I have come to fulfil the law; therefore it hath an end.
>
> Behold, I do not destroy the prophets, for as many as have not been fulfilled in me, verily I say unto you, shall all be fulfilled.
>
> And because I said unto you that old things have passed away, I do not destroy that which hath been spoken concerning things which are to come.
>
> For behold, the covenant which I have made with my people is not all fulfilled; but the law which was given unto Moses hath an end in me.
>
> Behold, I am the law, and the light. Look unto me, and endure to the end, and ye shall live; for unto him that endureth to the end will I give eternal life. (3 Nephi 15:4-9.)

Since this statement was made following the Savior's ministry among the Jews, and because there was a long period of apostasy following his ministry and that of his chosen Apostles in Jerusalem, it is logical that the Old Testament prophecies were directed to the Restoration of the latter days. This is explained by the Prophet Joseph Smith:

The time has at last arrived when the God of Abraham, of Isaac, and of Jacob, has set his hand again the second time to recover the remnants of his people, which have been left from Assyria, and from Egypt, and from Pathros, and from Cush, and from Elam, and from Shinar, and from Hamath, and from the islands of the sea, and with them to bring in the fulness of the Gentiles, and establish that covenant with them, which was promised when their sins should be taken away. See Isaiah 11; Romans 11:25, 26, and 27, and also Jeremiah 31:31, 32, and 33. This covenant has never been established with the house of Israel, nor with the house of Judah, for it requires two parties to make a covenant, and those two parties must be agreed, or no covenant can be made.

Christ, in the days of His flesh, proposed to make a covenant with them, but they rejected Him and His proposals, and in consequence thereof, they were broken off, and no covenant was made with them at that time. But their unbelief has not rendered the promise of God of none effect: no, for there was another day limited in David, which was the day of His power; and then His people, Israel, should be a willing people;—and He would write His law in their hearts, and print it in their thoughts; their sins and their iniquities He would remember no more.

Thus after this chosen family had rejected Christ and His proposals, the heralds of salvation said to them, 'Lo we turn unto the Gentiles'; and the Gentiles received the covenant, and were grafted in from whence the chosen family were broken off; but the Gentiles have not continued in the goodness of God, but have departed from the faith that was once delivered to the Saints, and have broken the covenant in which their fathers were established (see Isaiah 24:5); and have become highminded, and have not feared; therefore, but few of them will be gathered with the chosen family. Have not the pride, highmindedness, and unbelief of the Gentiles, provoked the Holy One of Israel to withdraw His Holy Spirit from them, and send forth His judgments to scourge them for their wickedness? This is certainly the case.[3]

The Savior also taught that when the words of Isaiah should be fulfilled, then the covenant which the Father had made unto the house of Israel would be fulfilled (see 3 Nephi 16:11, 17; 20:11-12). This covenant was originally made with Abraham and passed on through Isaac and through Jacob, whose name was changed to Israel. That the covenant of Abraham is being fulfilled today through The Church of Jesus Christ of Latter-day Saints is confirmed repeatedly in the Doctrine and Covenants (see 103:17; 124:58; 132:30-32).

A fourth reason for holding a symposium on Isaiah and the prophets is the most important one: by doing so, we obey the Savior's commandment to search these prophecies. To the Nephites he said:

> And now, behold, I say unto you, that ye ought to search these things. Yea, a commandment I give unto you that ye search these things diligently; for great are the words of Isaiah.
>
> For surely he spake as touching all things concerning my people which are of the house of Israel; therefore it must needs be that he must speak also to the Gentiles.
>
> And all things that he spake have been and shall be, even according to the words which he spake. (3 Nephi 23:1-3.)

As Isaiah is the only book in the Bible which the Savior singled out and commanded his people to search, we have designated this symposium "Isaiah and the Prophets." One of the major reasons for our searching the book of Isaiah is that we may study the testimony which it bears of Jesus Christ. Nephi quoted Isaiah that he "might more fully persuade them [his people] to believe in the Lord their Redeemer" (1 Nephi 19:23). Of the 425 separate verses of Isaiah quoted in the Book of Mormon, 391 or 92 percent of those verses say something about Christ. This illustrates the importance of the message of Isaiah. That Isaiah's teachings concerning the house of Israel and the Gentiles refer to these latter days is confirmed by the Savior's commentaries on the Isaiah passages in the Book of Mormon, and by the articles appearing in this volume. That "all things that he spake have been and shall be, even according to the words which he spake," was substantiated by the Jewish historian Josephus:

> He was, by the confession of all, a divine and wonderful man in speaking truth; and out of the assurance that he had never written what was false, he wrote down all his prophecies, and left them behind him in books, that their accomplishment might be judged of from the events by posterity.[4]

Despite this emphasis on Isaiah, a study of his writings alone is insufficient. The Savior extended his commandment to search Isaiah to include the rest of the prophets: "Search the prophets, for many there be that testify of these things" (3 Nephi 23:5). Such a search will furnish a second witness to Isaiah's great teachings concerning the house of Israel. Several of these supporting prophets are discussed in chapters of this book.

Many of the prophets ministered around the time of the captivity of the ten and one-half tribes of Israel by the Assyrians. This period of approximately fifty years (750-700 B.C.) was the time of the prophet Isaiah. Micah, Hosea, and Amos were other contemporary witnesses against the wickedness and evil practices which led to the destruction and captivity of this northern nation of Palestine. Joel and Jonah may also have prophesied during this period, but the dating of their work is much more controversial. All of these prophets carry a message which confirms what Isaiah had declared. Micah warns of the Lamanites' treading down the Gentiles who do not repent in the latter days. Hosea foretells the latter-day gathering of the house of Israel in the context of strange marriages and gives special emphasis to Ephraim. After chastising the children of Israel for their social sins, Amos predicts the latter-day famine of the Lord's word and the restoration of those who have been sifted as corn among all the nations of the earth. Joel speaks of the Spirit being poured out upon all flesh (which prophecy the angel Moroni said in 1823 was soon to be fulfilled), and also describes the Gentiles gathered together against the Jews in the valley of decision. Jonah's great message of God's love for all mankind is certainly applicable to us in this day of strife.

The next time period of the prophets is that of the captivity of Jerusalem by the Babylonians, when many Jews were carried into exile in Babylon (607 B.C. is the traditional biblical dating). Ezekiel and Daniel were the two prophets raised up to guide the captive Jews while they were separated from their homeland. Included in Ezekiel's extensive visions was the restoration of the two nations of the house of Israel, Judah and Ephraim (or Northern Israel), to one fold under one shepherd through the combining of the Book of Mormon and the Bible. He also foresaw many other aspects of the Restoration, as well as the great battle of Gog and Magog in the last days. Daniel interpreted King Nebuchadnezzar's dream, which showed the kingdom of God being set up in the latter days and being prepared and presented to the Son of Man by Adam, the Ancient of Days. The Latter-day Saints know that this great event will take place in the valley of Adam-ondi-Ahman.

Before and after the Jewish exiles were taken away, there were prophets throughout the land of Judah warning the people of the oncoming invasion of Babylon. Foremost among these prophets was the oft-persecuted Jeremiah. His life is a prime example of the Savior's declaration in the Sermon on the Mount that "so persecuted they the prophets which were before you" (Matthew 5:12). Jeremiah's "many prophecies," so labeled by Nephi, included several that are being fulfilled in our day. The Lord is taking "one of a city, and two of a family," and bringing them to Zion (Jeremiah 3:14). He is also sending forth many fishers and many hunters to accomplish a greater gathering than when the children of Israel were brought out of Egypt (see Jeremiah 16:14-16). The new covenant has been made with the house of Israel and will undoubtedly soon be made with the house of Judah, as Jeremiah prophesied (see Jeremiah 31:31-34). The prophets Habakkuk, Obadiah, and Zephaniah were also prophesying at this same time (approximately 630-580 B.C.). Although Obadiah's writings are not lengthy, to him is ascribed the well-known prophecy that "saviours shall come up on mount Zion" (Obadiah 1:21). One turns to Zephaniah to learn of events preceding the second coming of the Lord and the return of a pure language to the people of the Lord (see Zephaniah 3:1-9).

The scriptures are silent for a brief time, until the decree of Cyrus allows the Jews to return to their beloved homeland (538 B.C. is the traditional date of the decree). Then the Lord raises up two prophets, Haggai and Zechariah, to inspire the people to rebuild Jerusalem and the holy temple. While Haggai's message is basically to inspire his people to build the temple, he does speak of the coming of the mortal Messiah as "the desire of all nations" (Haggai 2:7). Such is not the case with Zechariah; his message extends to both comings of Jesus Christ and graphically predicts the Messiah's appearance to the Jews when all nations are gathered against the latter-day nation of Judah (see Zechariah 12:9-10; 13:6; 14:1-9). This prophecy is reiterated in the Doctrine and Covenants (see D&C 45:48-53). The last of the prophets comes to us again after a long period of no writings (some one hundred years, about 400 B.C.). Malachi, however, does not leave us wanting for prophecies about the latter days. Latter-day Saints are thrilled with his prophetic utterances of the messenger of the covenant to precede the Lord's coming in judgment upon the world, of his promise and warnings to latter-day Israel regarding the payment of tithes and offerings, and of the necessity of the coming of Elijah (which the Saints announce has been fulfilled). His writings also contain other choice items for those who will search the prophets.

Many people are reluctant to read the Old Testament because of its length and because they do not know the history and the background of the peoples. Perhaps a few facts will allay their fears. In the new LDS edition of the Bible, there are 1184 pages in the Old Testament; 860 of these pages precede the writings of the prophets. This leaves 324 pages from Isaiah to Malachi, but because these include many footnotes and cross-references, there are even fewer pages of actual text to read. This may not seem significant until it is realized that there are more pages in the New Testament, 403, than in the Old Testament prophets. That is, there are 79 fewer pages in the writings of these prophets than in the New Testament, making the prophets' writings only 80 percent as voluminous as the New Testament. Furthermore, although Isaiah and his contemporaries began their work around 750 B.C., the actual time covered by their writings is quite short. Two major time periods of only fifty years each include all the prophets' writing except the last three included in the present-day Bible. It does not seem too great a task to become acquainted with the historical and cultural background of these two brief time periods. This task should be enhanced by a knowledge of the great rewards that will result from such a study.

These two time periods should be of special interest to Latter-day Saints because of their relevance to us as a people. The first, the time preceding and following the capture of the ten tribes, is the history of our ancestors. Ephraim is the birthright tribe and therefore the spiritual leader of the house of Israel. After the division of Israel into two nations, following the reign of Solomon, the Northern Kingdom was known by the name of Ephraim. As the ten tribes were taken into the north, Ephraim particularly was scattered among the nations of the earth. Today Ephraim is being gathered out. Thus, a study of this time period is a study of our people.

The second time period is of equal importance. During that

fifty-year period, the prophet Lehi was called out of Jerusalem; he and his partner in travel, Ishmael, represented both tribes of Joseph, Manasseh and Ephraim, unto whom this great land of the Americas was given (see 3 Nephi 15:12-13). The land from which they left and the land to which they traveled constitute the two lands of promise where the house of Israel will be gathered. Learning the background of Palestine acquaints one with the prophecies regarding the future gathering to that land. The Old Testament prophets also uttered many prophecies regarding Zion, the other land of gathering. The Prophet Joseph Smith taught that Zion included the entire American continent:

> You know there has been great discussion in relation to Zion —where it is, and where the gathering of the dispensation is, and which I am now going to tell you. The prophets have spoken and written upon it; but I will make a proclamation that will cover a broader ground. *The whole of America is Zion itself from north to south, and is described by the Prophets, who declare that it is the Zion where the mountain of the Lord should be, and that it should be in the center of the land.* When Elders shall take up and examine the old prophecies in the Bible, they will see it.[5]

Thus the second time period should also hold a special interest for us in the latter days.

The other brief time periods covered by the writings of the last three prophets in the Bible may not be as significant to our day historically, but these writings certainly do contain prophecies of latter-day events which are doctrinally significant to us.

If we will keep the commandment to search the prophecies of Isaiah and these other prophets, we will agree with the pronouncement of Jesus that "great are the words of Isaiah" and that "many there be that testify of these things" (3 Nephi 23:1-5).

Notes

1. *Teachings of the Prophet Joseph Smith,* sel. Joseph Fielding Smith (Salt Lake City: Deseret Book Company, 1938), pp. 180-81.

2. Ibid., p. 181.

3. Ibid., pp. 14-15.

4. Flavius Josephus, *Josephus: Complete Works,* trans. William Whiston (Grand Rapids, Mich.: Kregel Publications, 1972), *Antiquities of the Jews* 10.2.2.

5. *Teachings of the Prophet Joseph Smith,* p. 362.

1

Joseph Smith as Found in Ancient Manuscripts

Joseph F. McConkie

This paper may be mistitled. Rather than "Joseph Smith as Found in Ancient Manuscripts" it ought to be "Joseph Smith as Lost in Ancient Manuscripts." Certainly the scriptures have proved themselves an excellent hiding place for things in which we express an interest but really lack the zeal to pursue. For most of us, this is particularly true of things in the Old Testament. My brief excursions into this ancient record leave me convinced that many of its greatest treasures rest undisturbed. A distinguished explorer in the mid-nineteenth century carried out a trial dig at the site of Jericho, and missed—by only a few yards—an ancient city wall which made headlines when discovered by another archaeologist a hundred years later. How often, in our own study of the scriptures and in our efforts to teach them, have we in like manner dug "dry holes" while piling our diggings on top of the very treasures we have sought?

If we as Latter-day Saints are to be successful in our search for the hidden treasures of the ancient scriptures, we must first succeed in finding the treasures of our modern scriptures. It is in the revelations of the Restoration that we obtain familiarity with principles of truth which, in turn, enhance our ability to recognize those same truths as they have been hidden in the succinct, spare, and often cryptic style of the Bible. The key to the revelations of the past is the revelations of the present, simply because the principles are eternal.

The basic thesis of this paper is that the ancients saw our day and knew of our prophets just as well as we can see their day and know of their prophets. As we know of Adam, Enoch, Noah, Abraham, and Moses, so they knew of Joseph Smith. As we are blessed by a knowledge of the past, so they were blessed by a knowledge of the future. It was by revelation that they understood the future, and it is by scripture that we understand the past. We know by modern revelation that certain of the ancient prophets knew of the Prophet Joseph Smith and described his future labors. This paper will seek to expand our known list of those who enjoyed such foreknowledge, and to introduce some interesting legends and traditions of antiquity about a latter-day prophet to be named Joseph. They are in surprising harmony with restored prophecies and events of our day.

The Restoration of All Things Spoken by All the Prophets

In identifying the time of the Second Coming, Peter said that it would follow the "restitution of all things, which God hath spoken by the mouth of all his holy prophets since the world began" (Acts 3:21). What is difficult to determine in this passage is whether Peter is saying that all that was spoken by the prophets about the last days will be restored before Christ comes, or that all the holy prophets knew that there would be a restoration of all things before the Second Coming. My preference is for the second interpretation, that all the holy prophets knew that there was to be a restoration of all things. This is not to say that all the prophets had the same degree of understanding. Abinadi illustrated this principle when he said "all the prophets" who had "prophesied ever since the world began" had spoken "more or less" concerning the coming of Christ (Mosiah 13:33). I would argue in like manner that all the holy prophets knew "more or less" of the universal restoration that was to precede the return of Christ, and that thus all the prophets knew "more or less" of the role of the Prophet Joseph Smith.

In so asserting I find myself in good company. Wilford Woodruff said there was "not one" of the ancient prophets who did not see and prophesy "about the great Zion of God in the latter days." Further he said:

And when we say this of them, we say it of every Apostle and Prophet who ever lived upon the earth. Their revelations and prophecies all point to our day and that great kingdom of God which was spoken of by Daniel, that great Zion of God spoken of by Isaiah and Jeremiah, and that great gathering of the house of Israel spoken of by Ezekiel and Malachi and many of the ancient Patriarchs and Prophets.[1]

From the days of father Adam to the last prophet of dispensations past has come a "mighty flood of prophecy" which, like a "strong band," has surrounded the Prophet Joseph Smith, dictating the great work that he would do. Such decrees had to be fulfilled to the very letter, and so it has been. "These mighty prophecies," Elder Woodruff avowed, were like a "band of iron [which] governed and controlled Joseph Smith in his labors."[2]

The Testimony of Adam and Enoch

In the great conference of the Church at Adam-ondi-Ahman, father Adam "stood up in the midst of the congregation; and . . . predicted whatsoever should befall his posterity unto the latest generation" (D&C 107:56). These prophecies were preserved in the book of Enoch, which book we do not now have but will yet. Joseph Smith did restore for us an extract of the record kept by Enoch. Among other things it contains a brief but clear description of the latter-day restoration of the gospel, including the coming forth of the Book of Mormon, the spreading of the gospel throughout the earth, the gathering of the elect, and the building of a "New Jerusalem" (Moses 7:62). Enoch, it will be recalled, was a contemporary of Adam's, having been ordained by him, and he was personally present when Adam made his remarkable prophecies (see D&C 107:48, 53). Yet Enoch's knowledge of these things was independent of his hearing them from father Adam, for "the Lord showed Enoch all things, even unto the end of the world" (Moses 7:67).

Although this gets us a little ahead of our story, it could be noted at this point that the apocryphal Hebrew Book of Enoch, also called Third Enoch, mentions a latter-day prophet who is to be involved in all these events. He is even named. As one would anticipate, his name is Joseph. He is referred to as the Messiah ben Joseph, *Messiah* meaning "anointed one" and *ben* meaning "son of." So what we have here in our first introduction to this tradition is a prophet son of Joseph of Egypt coming on the scene to play a dominant role in these latter-day events. In this work Enoch, seeing in vision the end of time, says: "I saw Messiah, son of Joseph, and his generation and their works and their doings that they will do against the nations of the world" (Hebrew Book of Enoch 45:5). Hugo Odeberg, who translated this work, observes that "the end of the course of the present world is marked by the appearance of Messiah ben Joseph and Messiah ben David, in whose times there will be wars between Israel and 'Gog and Magog'; the final consummation will then, so it seems, be brought about by the Holy One Himself."[3] A passage in another Enoch book is also linked to this tradition. Again the context is a depiction of world history, this time with animals used to symbolize men. Enoch narrates:

> And I saw that a white bull was born, with large horns, and all the beasts of the field and birds of the air feared him and made petition to him continually. And I saw till all their kinds were transformed, and they all became white cattle. And the foremost among them was the buffalo, and that buffalo was a great animal, and had great black horns on its head. And the Lord of the sheep rejoiced over them, and over all the cattle.[4]

All interpreters agree that the white bull represents the David Messiah, while the buffalo (wild ox) immediately brings to mind the blessing given to Joseph in Deuteronomy 33:13-17. The great horns with which the bullock is to push Israel together are "the emblem of Messiah ben Joseph" according to *The Jewish Encyclopedia*.[5] Of this Enoch passage Charles Torrey writes:

> It thus seems assured, beyond any reasonable doubt, that the "great animal" of Enoch 90:38, destined to appear in the very last days, is the Messiah ben Joseph. It is not by accident that the words with which he is introduced, "and the foremost among them (the cattle) was the buffalo," repeat the beginning of Deut. 33:17: "The firstling of his herd, . . . his horns are the horns of the wild-ox." The author of Enoch, who knew the Jewish tradition, intended by his "buffalo" the divine-human scion of Joseph's house. With the buffalo, yet above him, stood the white bull, the Anointed One of David's line; "and the Lord of the sheep rejoiced over them both."[6]

Joseph of Egypt Names Joseph Smith

Sensing the nearness of death, Joseph, following the pattern of his father Jacob, gathered his family around him. "I die," said Joseph to his assembled posterity. It is at this point in the story that the Joseph Smith Translation provides a marvelous restoration of text, completing the quotation of Joseph: "I die, *and go unto my fathers; and I go down to my grave with joy*" (JST, Genesis 50:24; italics added). Then this restored text goes on to give us an abbreviated account of Joseph's great prophecy of the destiny of his family and their role in the events of the last days, including the naming and describing of his son many generations removed, the Prophet Joseph Smith.

As Joseph, now an aged patriarch, prophetically unfolded the events that lay in the immediate future for Israel, he told his family how these events were but the pattern or foretelling of events of the last days. Seeing Israel's more immediate bondage to the Egyptians and their deliverance by a prophet of God as a parallel to their bondage to darkness in the last days and their deliverance once again by a heaven-sent servant, he wove the two stories together as one. The cycle of events common to both stories included Israel's prophesied bondage and the coming of a prophet who was to gather, liberate, and lead them. These liberator-prophets were not to be confused with the Messiah, Joseph cautioned, for they would be his servants. They were to be seers, revelators of gospel law, each foreknown by name. Each would write the words of the Lord and declare them with the aid of a spokesman.

Joseph identified the prophet of the Egyptian deliverance as Moses, and his spokesman as Aaron. He then rejoiced in the promise of a prophet to his own seed in the last days. To Joseph of Egypt the Lord said:

> I will remember you from generation to generation; and his name shall be called Joseph, and it shall be after the name of his father; and he shall be like unto you; for the thing which the Lord shall bring forth by his hand shall bring my people unto salvation. (JST, Genesis 50:33.)

This latter-day Joseph, then, according to the ancient prophecy, was to be like Moses and Joseph of Egypt. Thus again we see

Joseph's sense of history repeating itself in his telling of the story. There would be much in the life of the latter-day Joseph that would parallel his own. Indeed, the points of similarity are remarkable. For the present moment we note only that both were seers, both did a great labor for their families, both confounded their enemies, and as the ancient Joseph had become a temporal savior to the house of Israel, so the latter-day Joseph would become the source of spiritual salvation to Israel in the last days. Both were revelators and brought forth the word of the Lord, and both testified to having seen the Lord (see JST, Genesis 50:24).

At what point the knowledge of this prophecy was lost to Israel we do not know, but that it existed down through the days of Isaiah and even to the time of Jeremiah is certain, because it was from this time period that Lehi and his family obtained the brass plates from Laban which contained this prophecy. Lehi repeated much of the prophecy to his son Joseph. Of that Nephi said: "And the prophecies which he [Joseph of Egypt] wrote, there are not many greater. And he prophesied concerning us, and our future generations; and they are written upon the plates of brass" (2 Nephi 4:2). This statement is in harmony with the JST account of Joseph's prophecy, which concludes, "And Joseph confirmed many other things unto his brethren" (JST, Genesis 50:37). It is evident that, in both the old world and the new, much more was known about the events of the last days and the role of the Prophet Joseph Smith than has been preserved for us.

The Name Joseph and Its Ancient Meaning

The prophecy of Jacob's son Joseph that the latter-day seer would bear his name, and that it would also be the name of his father, is commonly known in the Church. What is not generally understood is the need for the Prophet to bear a particular name—and if a particular name, why the name Joseph?

In patriarchal times personal names were considered to be of the greatest importance. Conscious effort was made to assure identity between the name and its bearer. Given names often constituted a miniature biography of the bearer. Names were used as reminders of significant events, to connote character, to identify position, and in some instances to foreshadow the bearer's destiny or that of his posterity; that is, as memorials, as symbols, and as prophecies.

Among righteous people, names were used to identify and testify of great truths or great events, thus keeping such things constantly in the consciousness of the people.

The etymology of the name Joseph is usually given as "the Lord addeth" or "increaser." Though appropriate, such renderings have veiled a richer meaning associated with the name. In Genesis 30:24, where Rachel names her infant son Joseph, the Hebrew text reads "Asaph," which means "he who gathers," "he who causes to return," or perhaps most appropriately, "God gathereth." Thus the great prophet of the Restoration was given the name that most appropriately describes his divine calling.

Having learned of the special meaning associated with the Prophet's name, I was especially interested when I discovered the following in the patriarchal blessing of the Prophet's older brother Hyrum. "Behold thou art Hyrum, the Lord hath called thee by that name, and by that name He has blessed thee."[7] It then dawned on me that Hyrum is also a Hebrew name which means "my brother is exalted." What more appropriate name could have been given to the man who was destined to go with Joseph to Carthage and seal his testimony with his blood? So the testimony of the Restoration has been sealed on this dispensation with the blood of two prophets who, according to the ancient tradition, bore the right names.

Joseph Smith as Known to Isaiah

No Bible prophet has had more to say about the restoration of the gospel and the gathering of Israel in our dispensation than Isaiah. In chapter 11 Isaiah speaks of the gathering of both Ephraim (typifying the northern kingdom) and Judah (representing the southern kingdom), and of the eventual peace that will exist between them. The story is told in prophetic imagery using a "stem," a "rod," and a "root" to represent key figures. In a revelation to Joseph Smith (D&C 113) the "stem of Jesse" is identified as Jesus Christ. The imagery is most excellent—the "slender twig shooting out from the trunk of an old tree, cut down, lopped to the very root, and decayed; which tender plant, so weak in appearance, should nevertheless become fruitful and prosper."[8] So Isaiah affirms for us that the Messiah was to come of the house of Jesse, as a shoot or branch which would bear good fruit. Our explanatory modern revelation identifies the "rod" in the prophecy as "a servant in the hands of Christ, who is partly a descendant of Jesse as well as of Ephraim, or of the house of Joseph, on whom there is laid much power" (D&C 113:4). No further explanation is given. It has always been our understanding in the Church that the passage applies to Joseph Smith, this being one of the reasons it was quoted to him by Moroni in September 1823. By way of explanation as to who the "root" is, the revelation declares: "It is a descendant of Jesse, as well as of Joseph, unto whom rightly belongs the priesthood, and the keys of the kingdom, for an ensign, and for the gathering of my people in the last days" (D&C 113:6). There can be no question that this is describing the Prophet Joseph Smith. By revelation he was told that he held the right to the priesthood (see D&C 86:8-9). That the keys of the kingdom had been given to him is a matter of record; that his labors were to stand as an "ensign" to which the nations of the earth will gather is also a matter of scriptural promise (D&C 29:4, 7-8; 35:25; 38:33; 39:11; 45:9, 28).

Isaiah 29 contains what was, as originally recorded, an amazingly detailed account of the coming forth of the Book of Mormon and its translation at the hands of an "unlearned" prophet. Only a fragment of the original prophecy has survived, but even this is sufficient for the reader to know that in a period of universal apostasy, a time when men are spiritually asleep, having no prophets or seers, the words of a book would be taken to a "learned" man to read and he would say "I cannot; for it is sealed." Then the book is given "to him that is not learned," and through his labors the words of the book go forth so that the spiritually blind can "see out of obscurity, and out of darkness." Thus among a people thinking themselves learned would the Lord accomplish "a marvellous work and a wonder" which would cause the wisdom of their wise men to perish (Isaiah 29:9-22).

A more meaningful and detailed account of Isaiah's prophecy has been preserved for us in 2 Nephi 27. Here Nephi clearly identifies the context of this prophecy as "the last days," or "the days of the Gentiles," a time when men upon "all the lands of the earth" would be "drunken with iniquity and all manner of abominations." It would be a time, Nephi tells us, when men would have deliberately "closed [their] eyes" to truth and would have rejected the teachings of "the prophets." At such a time the unlearned prophet would bring forth a book containing the testimony of those who "have slumbered." This book, which would contain "a revelation from God, from the beginning of the world to the ending thereof," would remain partially sealed because of the wickedness of men. Yet in the due time of the Lord even that portion of the book that is sealed will be brought forth, and the secret acts of all men will be revealed.

That Isaiah 11 and 29 contain direct references to Joseph Smith is generally known to Latter-day Saints. Building upon that knowledge, I would like to suggest that Isaiah 49, one of the "suffering servant" prophecies, also described Joseph Smith and his role as the great prophet of the latter-day restoration. In Judaism this prophecy is viewed as describing the suffering of the nation of the Jews. Among the so-called Christian world, it has traditionally been interpreted as a description of the life and ministry of Christ. While Latter-day Saints accept the traditional Christian interpretation, let us now consider the possibility that this prophecy may have still another application.

The Book of Mormon translation of this chapter contains some helpful additions to the standard Bible text. We will freely draw on them in our brief summary of the chapter. The introductory verse is effectually a warning voice to Israel, which is scattered among every nation, kindred, and tongue—they are told to give heed to the voice of the Lord as he speaks through the mouth of his servant. The servant is to declare that "the Lord hath called me from the womb; from the bowels of my mother hath he made mention of my name." So we look for a prophet, one declaring his own fore-ordination, with the added claim that his name was known to Israel even before his birth. Could we assume that, as Israel knew the name of the prophet who was to liberate them from their Egyptian bondage, they also knew the name of the prophet who would "bring them out of darkness into light; out of hidden darkness, and out of captivity unto freedom" (JST, Genesis 50:25) in that day when they were scattered among all the nations of the earth? Could it be that this was the prophet who was to be like unto Moses? (See JST, Genesis 50:29.)

Surely it is more than coincidence that Doctrine and Covenants section 1, the revelation given by the Lord to introduce the compilation of revelations declaring authority to gather Israel, would use the very language of Isaiah to introduce Joseph Smith and the Restoration (see D&C 1:1; cf. Isaiah 49:1). Joseph Smith had already given to the world a restoration of the prophecy by Joseph of Egypt that his name was once known to Israel (see 2 Ne. 3:15), and he later declared that he was "ordained from before the foundation of the world for some good end, or bad, as you may choose to call it" (D&C 127:2).

Isaiah then gives us the words with which this messenger to scattered Israel is to characterize himself: "And he hath made my mouth like a sharp sword," he is to say, and "in the shadow of his hand he hid me, and made me a polished shaft; in his quiver hath he hid me."

We look for a servant who will come as one having authority, who will speak in the name of God, as did the Prophet Joseph Smith, saying, "Give heed unto my word, which is quick and powerful, sharper than a two-edged sword, to the dividing asunder of both joints and marrow; therefore give heed unto my words" (D&C 6:2). Joseph Smith declared himself to be a literal descendant of Joseph of Egypt. Of his lineage, the Lord said he had been "hid from the world with Christ in God" (D&C 86:9). And of himself Joseph Smith said the following:

> I am like a huge, rough stone rolling down from a high mountain; and the only polishing I get is when some corner gets rubbed off by coming in contact with something else, striking with accelerated force against religious bigotry, priestcraft, lawyer-craft, doctor-craft, lying editors, suborned judges and jurors, and the authority of perjured executives, backed by mobs, blasphemers, licentious and corrupt men and women—all hell knocking off a corner here and a corner there. Thus I will become a smooth and polished shaft in the quiver of the Almighty, who will give me dominion over all and every one of them, when their refuge of lies shall fail, and their hiding place shall be destroyed, while these smooth-polished stones with which I come in contact become marred.[9]

Isaiah 49:3 refers to this prophet in terms of a composite person —one who typifies or represents all of faithful Israel. It naturally follows that if there is a prophet of destiny there must of necessity be a people of destiny. Both prophet and people are servants of the

Lord. In the collective body of the people are found the attributes of their leader, his life, works, and character constituting a profile of his people. Isaiah delineates the chosen servant's mission and office thus: (1) he was called of God (49:1); (2) he was prepared from before the foundations of the earth (49:1); (3) he was known by name even before his birth (49:1); (4) he was the one who would restore Israel (49:5-6); (5) he would teach true religion to all nations (49:6); (6) he would be the embodiment of the new covenant (49:8); and (7) his labors, like those of the Master, would be accomplished in humiliation and suffering (50:4-7; 52:13-15). As it was with the prophet, so it would be with his people. They too must have been called of God, ordained to their earthly mission even before birth, destined to be of Israel and of the house of Joseph, and willing, despite humiliation and suffering, to go to the ends of the earth to declare the message of salvation and gather Israel once more to new and everlasting covenants.

In verses 4 and 5 of Isaiah 49 our prophet character assumes the profile of a suffering servant, lamenting to the heavens that he has labored in vain, then receives the promise of the Lord that he will yet come off triumphant. One need only read the pleas to the Lord written by Joseph Smith while a prisoner in the Liberty Jail to see how perfectly these passages describe both his circumstances and his feelings.

In these verses we have returned to the description of an individual servant, yet the individual is still the personification of what Israel is to be collectively. As he has been endowed with power from on high, so Israel when restored to her ancient priesthood and covenants will be endowed with heavenly power; as their leader triumphs over humiliation, so they as a nation will ultimately triumph.

I will not attempt to detail the prophecy from this point. Let it suffice that it speaks of the servant-prophet's role in gathering Israel and taking the gospel to the Gentiles—both of which accomplishments, we might note, went beyond the role of the earthly ministry of the Savior. It speaks of our prophet as being despised and abhorred by the great and noble of the earth, and yet of a time when such will humbly seek after his message. This prophecy even extends the teaching of the gospel to those on the other side of the veil, indicating that the prophet's authority will reach even to them. It speaks of the gathering of Israel in great numbers to the mountains of the Lord and to the lands of their inheritance.

To those who would argue that Isaiah 49 has nothing to do with the Prophet Joseph Smith, I must concede they may be right. Yet I would feel a bit like the rabbi who, when confronted with the archaeologist's arguments that there was no Moses, agreed that Moses may not have existed, but that if he did not, he undoubtedly had a cousin called Moses who did everything Moses was said to have done. If Isaiah 49 is not a description of Joseph Smith, then I anxiously wait for another to appear on the scene and do exactly what Joseph Smith did.

Jeremiah's Prophecy of an Ephraimite Prophet

Leaving Isaiah, may I now suggest that Jeremiah described both Joseph Smith and the First Vision. I take no credit for seeing what others have not seen; I got the idea from an old Jewish writer who, after reading a passage from Jeremiah, announced, "Certainly we could not blame any Jew who should see in these words a Messiah ben Joseph."[10] He then added that the passage was to be fulfilled in the last days. After careful examination I decided my old Jewish friend was right; Jeremiah was not one whit behind Isaiah and others of the ancient prophets in his ability to see and describe events of our day and in his knowledge of the Prophet Joseph Smith. The passage is Jeremiah 30:21, which in the King James Bible reads thus: "And their nobles shall be of themselves, and their governor shall proceed from the midst of them; and I will cause him to draw near, and he shall approach unto me: for who is this that engaged his heart to approach unto me? saith the Lord."

How is such a conclusion drawn from this passage? First, we must look to the context from which it comes. Jeremiah chapters 30 and 31 deal with the latter-day restoration of Israel. They form a unit and should be read together. By tradition they are known as the Book of Consolation, because of the solace they extended to Israel when the prospects of the nation were at their lowest. The testimony of these chapters is that there would again be a day when Israel would return to their lands and former glory, with prophets at their head and the favor of God resting upon them. To this they are to look, and in this they are to believe. That Jeremiah's prophecy was not fulfilled in their return from the

Babylonian captivity is evident from the prominent role he ascribes to Ephraim in these chapters. He clearly identifies Ephraim as the tribe of the birthright and as the moving force behind the gathering. This certainly has not been the case in any instance before our day. Ephraim is described as "the watchmen upon the mount," the tribe designated to raise the warning voice, to gather Israel, and to declare the word of the Lord. Ephraim repented and was instructed in the principles of salvation (see Jeremiah 31:19). The prophetic promise was that of a returning to the true and living God, of a restoration of ancient truths, and of "a new covenant," for the Lord said, "This shall be the covenant that I will make with the house of Israel; After those days . . . I will put my law in their inward parts, and write it in their hearts; and will be their God, and they shall be my people" (Jeremiah 31:33).

In that setting we return our attention to the passage in question. The old Jewish commentator quoted it thus: "His Mighty One shall proceed from himself and his Ruler come forth from his own midst."[11] Thus he is changing the plural "nobles" of the King James translation to the singular "Mighty One." This is in harmony with our more recent Bible translations.

For instance, the Jerusalem Bible reads:

> Their prince will be one of their own, their ruler come from their own people. I will let him come freely into my presence and he can come close to me; who else, indeed, would risk his life by coming close to me?—it is Yahweh who speaks.

The New English Bible reads:

> A ruler shall appear, one of themselves, a governor shall arise from their own number. I will myself bring him near and so he shall approach me; for no one ventures of himself to approach me, says the Lord."

Other possible renditions could be "their Glorious One" or "Leader."[12]

The passage promises a single "leader" from Ephraim who will be brought into the presence of the Lord Jehovah and then assume the presiding role in the latter-day gathering of Israel.

Messiah ben Joseph

As we have referred to the ancient tradition of a latter-day prophet—the Messiah ben Joseph, or ben Ephraim, as he is vari-

ously called—let us now consider that tradition and its origins. Old
Testament prophecies dealing with the coming of Christ naturally
divide themselves into those speaking of his earthly ministry and
those describing his second coming. In the literature of the Jews it
is not uncommon to find reference to the Messiah ben Joseph associated with the passages dealing with the earthly ministry of
Christ. These are often referred to as the "suffering servant"
passages. The nation longed for a triumphant king, one who would
free them from bondage and return them to the glory of David's
day. They could talk endlessly about those passages dealing with
their triumphant liberator. The passages dealing with Christ's
rejection, his being despised, bruised, and afflicted, and his being
"brought as a lamb to the slaughter" (Isaiah 53:7) caused them
considerably more difficulty, especially when the messianic flavor
of such passages was too obvious to be denied. (We are obviously
talking here about many of Isaiah's prophecies.) In an attempt to
resolve this difficulty, a well-established Jewish dogma of a second
messiah is cited—one destined to be a suffering messiah, a martyr
messiah, but not to be confused with their triumphant king. "The
doctrine of two Messiahs holds an important place in Jewish
theology," writes a Yale theologian, Charles Torrey, "more important and more widely attested than is now generally recognized. It
is not a theory imperfectly formulated or only temporarily held,
but a standard article of faith, early and firmly established and
universally accepted."[13] Briefly stated, the doctrine is this:
"According to a talmudic statement the Jews believed in two
Messiahs, one of the tribe of Joseph, or rather who was an
Ephraimite, and the other a scion of David."[14] The Messiah ben
Joseph, according to this tradition, is to be killed, following which
the Messiah ben David is to make his triumphant appearance. So
then the suffering servant passages could be handled by simply
being applied to the Messiah ben Joseph.

Excepting Samaritan sources, virtually every reference to the
Messiah ben Joseph notes his violent death. Since the Samaritans
believed themselves to be Ephraimites, they refused to admit the
possibility that their prophet-hero could be killed. The general
agreement, however, is that he was to die at the hands of the
enemies of Israel. Since he was to appear on the scene in the last

days, his death is most often associated with the battle of Arma-
geddon, when the forces of Gog and Magog march against the
gathered host of Israel. Though this is the generally accepted
tradition in later literature, it traces to secondary sources. The
earliest of sources that have survived to our day—these would be
the references to the Messiah ben Joseph in the Jerusalem and
Babylonian Talmuds—affirm his martyr's death, but do not mention the nature of it.

I would suggest that the best explanation of the manner of his
death is to be found in the Testament of Benjamin, the younger
brother of Joseph, in the Testaments of the Twelve Patriarchs.
Benjamin recounts the manner in which Joseph besought his
father to seek the Lord's forgiveness in behalf of his brothers for
their transgression against him, and how Jacob in turn announced
his knowledge of the special promise made to Joseph's seed. Benjamin says Joseph

> besought our father that he would pray for his brethren, that the
> Lord would not impute to them as sin whatever evil they had
> done unto him. And thus Jacob cried out: My good child, thou
> has prevailed over the bowels of thy father Jacob. And he em-
> braced him, and kissed him for two hours, saying: In thee shall
> be fulfilled the prophecy of heaven which says "that a
> blameless one shall be delivered up for lawless men, and a sin-
> less one shall die for ungodly men."[15]

After quoting this passage, H. J. Schonfield observed that "The
Patriarch Joseph does not really qualify as fulfiller of such a
prophecy; but he was regarded as the antetype of a righteous man
killed by the godless, a veritable suffering Ben Joseph."[16] Whether
the phrases "blameless" and "sinless" both have reference to
Messiah ben Joseph is open to question. It seems to me that the
"sinless" prophet who was to die "for ungodly men" could be
none other than Jesus Christ. The "blameless one" who was to die
at the hands of the "lawless men" is the Messiah ben Joseph. In
either case, the prophecy is a remarkable description of the death
of the Prophet Joseph Smith, who was murdered by a "lawless"
mob on June 27, 1844.

A number of interesting traditions surround the death of the
Messiah ben Joseph. One holds that after having restored temple

worship he would be killed. "Then the time of the last extreme suffering and persecution for Israel will begin, from which escape will be sought by flight into the wilderness."[17]

These events are closely associated with the return of Elijah, who is to restore the Messiah ben Joseph to life and join the righteous in their flight into the desert, where they are to remain until joined by the Messiah, who will then begin his redemptive work.[18]

Joseph's role in destroying the kingdoms of wickedness is also emphasized in a Jewish tradition about the blessings given by Jacob to his sons. Louis Ginzberg records that Jacob "called Benjamin a wolf, Judah a lion, and Joseph a bull" in order to

> point to the three kingdoms known as wolf, lion, and bull, and the doom of which was and will be sealed by the descendants of his three sons: Babylon, the kingdom of the lion, fell through the hands of Daniel of the tribe of Judah; Media, the wolf, found its master in the Benjamite Mordecai; and the bull Joseph will subdue the horned beast, the kingdom of wickedness, before the Messianic time.[19]

There is also a very old Jewish tradition that Edom or Idumea, meaning the powers of the world, can fall only at the hands of Joseph. One Jewish writer stated that it was the "province of the Messiah son of Joseph to conquer Israel's enemies."[20] These threads of tradition come from whole cloth. Doctrine and Covenants section 1, which, as we have already seen, introduces Joseph Smith in the language of Isaiah, picks up that language again to announce the imminent return of Christ: "Prepare ye, prepare ye for that which is to come, for the Lord is nigh; and the anger of the Lord is kindled, and his sword is bathed in heaven, and it shall fall upon the inhabitants of the earth" (D&C 1:12-13). Isaiah's exact language was: "For my sword shall be bathed in heaven: behold, it shall come down upon Idumea, and upon the people of my curse, to judgment" (Isaiah 34:5). The modern revelation continues (and we are paraphrasing Isaiah and Moses here):

> And the arm of the Lord shall be revealed; and the day cometh that they who will not hear the voice of the Lord, neither the voice of his servants, neither give heed to the words of the prophets and apostles, shall be cut off from among the people;
> For they have strayed from mine ordinances, and have broken mine everlasting covenant;

They seek not the Lord to establish his righteousness, but every man walketh in his own way, and after the image of his own god, whose image is in the likeness of the world, and whose substance is that of an idol, which waxeth old and shall perish in Babylon, even Babylon the great, which shall fall. (D&C 1:14-16.)

The revelation then announces that Joseph Smith has been given the power "to lay the foundation" of the Church, "to bring it forth out of obscurity and out of darkness," and to send forth to all men the message of repentance, for "the Lord shall have power over his saints, and shall reign in their midst, and shall come down in judgment upon Idumea, or the world" (vss. 30-36).

In summarizing the Messiah ben Joseph tradition, it should be said that his role centers in—in fact, he seems to be the focal point of—the latter-day gathering of Israel. In this role he is to restore true temple worship, return Judah to Palestine, rebuild the city of Jerusalem, build the temple there anew, and bring to pass the restoration of the ten tribes. All of this is destined to happen before the coming of the Messiah ben David. The Messiah ben Joseph tradition is always closely associated with the return of Elijah, who is also to be a forerunner of the Messiah. Elijah, according to such traditions, is "charged with the mission of ordering the coming time aright and restoring the tribes of Jacob."[21] It is believed that when Elijah comes he must adjust "all matters of law and Biblical interpretation" and correct "all genealogical records." He is to destroy the power of Satan and to be "instrumental in bringing Israel to genuine repentance," establishing peace, and turning the hearts of the fathers to the children and the hearts of the children to the fathers.[22] "Elijah's chief activity," it is stated, "will consist in restoring the purity of the family."[23]

The traditions also include a prophecy by Joseph's mother Rachel "that Joseph would be the ancestor of the (Ephraimitic) Messiah, who would arise at the end of days,"[24] along with an interesting variation on the dreams of his youth. According to such accounts "Joseph dreamed a dream, and he could not refrain from telling it to his brethren." In this dream he and his brothers were gathering fruit. "Your fruit rotted, but mine remained sound," Joseph explained. "Your seed will set up dumb images of idols, but they will vanish at the appearance of my descendant, the Messiah of Joseph."[25]

Origins of the Tradition

Perhaps as interesting as anything else in relationship to the Messiah ben Joseph traditions is the fact that no one seems to know where they came from. No passage in today's canon fits. Arguments have attempted to tie these traditions to Jacob's patriarchal blessing to Joseph, to the blessing given by Moses to the tribe of Joseph, to Isaiah's suffering servant passages, and, as we have seen, to Jeremiah's reference to an Ephraimite prophet. Other arguments have involved Ezekiel's prophecy about the stick of Joseph, Daniel's reference to "Messiah the Prince," and passages in Joel and Hosea which have been linked to the Teacher of Righteousness of the Dead Sea Scrolls, who has also been associated with the Messiah ben Joseph. Also, attempts have been made to associate the tradition with Obadiah's references to the leading role of the tribe of Joseph in the events of the last days; Habakkuk's reference to a prophet who would do a work that would cause men to "wonder marvelously," a work which most would not believe (which passage is especially interesting because Christ applied it to Joseph Smith in 3 Nephi 21); and Micah and Zechariah. The marvelous thing is that none of them fit. None of them speak of a prophet named Joseph who would be a son of Joseph of Egypt called to gather Israel in the last days.

To the Latter-day Saint the answer is simple. We have read it in the text that Joseph Smith restored to chapter 50 of Genesis in his translation and in 2 Nephi 3, where Lehi gives a patriarchal blessing to his son Joseph. But the scholars continue to be puzzled. Professor Torrey writes:

> Some biblical passage or picture, indeed, is to be looked for as the source of this remarkable feature of Jewish eschatology. It would seem to be beyond question that a tenet of such importance, well established in Talmud, Targum, and Midrash, must have its proof texts in canonical Hebrew scripture.[26]

In speaking of the idea of the two Messiahs, ben Joseph and ben David, he says:

> Here are two divinely anointed beings, each connected in the closest way with the fate of both Israel and the nations of the world. It is hardly possible to believe that the Rabbis could have adopted and given out this very significant article of faith merely on the basis of speculation, without definite prophetic authority.[27]

What Of It All

I will borrow for my conclusion the words I wrote in the book *His Name Shall Be Joseph,* which contains a more detailed discussion of the tradition of a Messiah ben Joseph and the knowledge had by the ancients of the Prophet Joseph Smith:

Only the light of the restored gospel can dispel the shadows of time and bring the tapestry of legend and tradition into full view. Only as we stand in that heavenly light that surrounded the youthful Joseph Smith as Moroni unfolded the mysteries of the ancient scriptures to him can we see as Joseph saw and as the prophets of all ages have seen. It takes a prophet to understand the prophetic. The revelations of the past are of little worth without revelation in the present. Until one shares the testimony of living revelation the arguments of past revelation are but the expressions of one who sees "through a glass darkly." One must have life to grant life. Only living revelation can grant life to the revelation of ages past. Having the revealed knowledge that Jacob's son, Joseph, did in fact have Heaven's promise that a latter-day descendant of his would yet bear his name and do again his work in restoring Israel, can we be blamed in seeing in such traditions a resemblance to truths once had? It is a resemblance far too close to have been born of chance. Even the frills of the folklorist, the embroideries of the Talmudist, and the gross exaggerations to which all ancient tales are subject have not destroyed that likeness. Our prophet bears the right name, he was of the right lineage, he was in reality anointed, he did the right works, he taught the right doctrines, and he died the violent death anticipated by the traditions. All of this he did without ever hearing of the legends of which we speak, and in doing so he stood singularly and uniquely alone among the religious leaders of the world. Not since the days of the Bible has there been one like him, and from among the world's religious leaders none have sought association with him.

In such legends and traditions we find fuel for testimony, but only if the fire of testimony already burns brightly. Such things can add to the burning fire but have no power in themselves to kindle that fire. They are not the source of testimony and thus have no profitable place in the proselyting efforts of the Church. They will not convert the Jew, though they may serve as an additional anchor to the converted Jew. They do not prove the verity of the Restoration and the prophetic mission of Joseph Smith, though as all things bear record of Christ, so they sustain our revealed testimony of the great Prophet of the Restoration. We would not and do not expect the world to see in these tradi-

tions that which we see in them. As the scriptures were used
anciently to reject the living Messiah, so they are used today to
reject the message of the Restoration. We cannot expect others
viewing the distant horizon of legend and tradition, and doing so
without the light of the new day, to see what we have seen. The
wealth of Messianic prophecies has not converted the Jew, and
the thousands of prophetic passages describing the Apostasy
and Restoration have not dissuaded the Christian. The Sad-
ducees and Pharisees are alive and well. But surely it does not
remain for people who have denied the Christ by tradition, by
creed, or by deed, and who have sealed the heavens, professing
that they cannot speak, to sit in judgment on those who have
found him and have heard his voice. As Joseph Smith asked,
"Does it remain for a people who never had faith enough to call
down one scrap of revelation from heaven . . . to say how much
God has spoken and how much he has not spoken?" (*History of
the Church* 2:18). Such traditions are but the rags of the past,
yet the rags evidence the whole cloth. They are but ashes, yet
the ashes evidence that once things burned with fervent heat.
They are but a skeleton, yet the skeleton evidences that there
was flesh and blood and spirit.[28]

Notes

1. *Journal of Discourses,* 26 vols. (London: Latter-day Saints' Book Depot, 1855-86), 16:264.

2. Ibid., p. 267.

3. Hugo Odeberg, trans., *3 Enoch or the Hebrew Book of Enoch* (reprint ed.; New York: KTAV Publishing House, 1973), p. 144.

4. R. H. Charles, *The Apocrypha and Pseudepigrapha of the Old Testament,* 2 vols. (Oxford: Clarendon Press, 1977), 2:260; also see Charles T. Torrey, "The Messiah Son of Ephraim," *Journal of Biblical Literature* 66 (1947):266-68.

5. *The Jewish Encyclopedia,* 12 vols. (New York: Funk and Wagnalls Company, 1904), 8:512.

6. Torrey, pp. 267-68.

7. Joseph Fielding Smith, *Origins of the "Reorganized" Church,* 4th ed. (Independence, Mo.: Zion's Printing and Publishing Co., 1945), p. 60. For additional commentary on names and their ancient significance see Joseph Fielding McConkie, *His Name Shall Be Joseph* (Salt Lake City: Hawkes Publications, 1980), pp. 154-58.

8. Adam Clarke, *The Holy Bible . . . with a Commentary and Critical Notes,* rev. ed., 6 vols. in 3 (Nashville: Abingdon, n.d.), 4:72.

9. Joseph Smith, *History of the Church of Jesus Christ of Latter-day Saints,* ed. B. H. Roberts, 7 vols. (Salt Lake City: Deseret Book Company, 1932-51), 5:401.

10. Edward G. King, trans., *The Yalkut on Zechariah* (Cambridge, England: Deighton, Bell and Co., 1882), p. 87.

11. Ibid.

12. David Brown, A. R. Fausset, and Robert Jamieson, *Commentary of the Whole Bible* (Grand Rapids, Mich.: Zondervan Publishing House, 1976), p. 633.

13. Torrey, p. 253.

14. Solomon Zeitlin, "The Essenes and Messianic Expectations," *Jewish Quarterly Review* 45 (1954):107.

15. Charles, 2:355-56.

16. H. J. Schonfield, *Secrets of the Dead Sea Scrolls* (New York: A. S. Barnes and Company, 1975), p. 71.

17. *The Jewish Encyclopedia* 1:683.

18. Louis Ginzberg, *The Legends of the Jews,* 7 vols. (Philadelphia: Jewish Publication Society of America, 1911), 6:340.

19. Ginzberg, 2:147.

20. Julius H. Greenstone, *The Messiah Idea in Jewish History* (Philadelphia: Jewish Publication Society of America, 1906), p. 320.

21. Ginzberg, 4:233.

22. Greenstone, p. 96.

23. Ginzberg, 6:339.

24. Ginzberg, 5:299; also see Raphael Patai, *The Messiah Texts* (New York: Avon Books, 1979), p. 165.

25. Ginzberg, 2:7.

26. Torrey, p. 257.

27. Ibid.

28. McConkie, pp. 180-81.

2

Temple Symbolism in Isaiah

John M. Lundquist

The main theme of this paper is the centrality of the theme of the temple in the book of Isaiah. From the time that the temple was dedicated by Solomon to the time it was destroyed by the Babylonians, its role in the spiritual life of the Judahite monarchy fluctuated wildly. It was, interestingly enough, within the reigns of the first and the last kings of Isaiah's tenure as prophet, Ahaz and Manasseh, that the temple's role was most abused. Ahaz, who was king of Judah when the Northern Kingdom was defeated by Assyria, introduced a large bronze altar that he had seen and admired in Damascus into the place on the temple platform that was occupied by the altar of burnt offerings (see 2 Kings 16). Manasseh, the king of Judah in whose reign Isaiah was martyred according to the pseudepigraphal Martyrdom of Isaiah,[1] introduced cult prostitution and star worship along the lines known to Phoenician religion into the temple in Jerusalem (see 2 Kings 21, 23).

It was during the reign of Hezekiah, approximately midway through Isaiah's long period of prophetic service, that the role of the temple in the religious life of Judah approached that which had been intended in the beginning. The king was intended to play a large and central role in the cultic life of Israel, as is made clear by the roles played by David and Solomon. As A. R. Johnson states, "The king is not only found leading his people in worship with the offering of the sacrifice and prayer on important occasions in the national life, but throughout the four hundred years of the Davidic dynasty, from the time of David's active concern for the ark to that of Josiah's thorough-going reform, himself superintends the organization of the cultus in all its aspects."[2] During the reign of Hezekiah, not only did the king fulfill his role more fully regarding the temple, but also the intended role between king and prophet was more fully realized than perhaps during any other period. It was at this time that Hezekiah laid the threatening letter from the king of Assyria "before the Lord" in the temple, that is, in the Holy of Holies, and prayerfully sought the Lord's help. In response to his prayer the Lord gave him the message of salvation from the Assyrian menace through the prophet Isaiah (see 2 Kings 19).

The most important illustration of the theme of the temple in the book of Isaiah is the description of Isaiah's extraordinary prophetic call through a glorious vision of the Lord in the Holy of Holies of the Jerusalem temple (see Isaiah 6).

What are the main themes relating to the temple that stand out in the book of Isaiah? In order to more fully answer this question, it is necessary that I digress momentarily in order to lay a more firm basis for understanding the role of the temple in Isaiah. Over the past year I have been engaged in research in which I have been attempting to identify the main features and symbols of temple worship in the ancient Near East, including Israel. I have concluded from this research that there was a common "temple ideology" in the ancient Near East, a common ritual language and practice that revolved around great temples and that would have been understood across language and cultural boundaries. One scholar has written that "if the temple ideologies of the different nations are able to display certain traits, common throughout the whole ancient world, it may be a special branch of the Chaos-Cosmos ideology."[3] Dr. Hugh Nibley has explained the probable reason behind such widespread diffusion of similar rites: the temple rites were revealed by God to the earliest parents of the human race, and from a center of earliest civilization spread to other centers by the dual processes of diffusion and usurpation. "Comparative studies . . . discovered the common pattern in all ancient religions," and "have also demonstrated the processes of *diffusion* by which that pattern was spread throughout the world—and in the process torn to shreds, of which recognizable remnants may be found in almost any land and time.''[4] What is the "pattern" that can be found "in almost any land and time"? In order for us to understand the role of the temple in Isaiah's writings, we must have some idea of what we are looking for. This is the "temple ideology" that I have mentioned, and it is this ideology that I have tried to delineate during my research of the past year. The following is my tentative attempt to identify this pattern:

The Temple: A Preliminary Typology

1. The temple is the architectural embodiment of the cosmic mountain.

2. The cosmic mountain represents the primordial hillock, the place which first emerged from the waters that covered the earth during the creative process. In Egypt, for example, all temples are seen as representing the primordial hillock.

3. The temple is often associated with the waters of life which flow from a spring within the building itself—or rather the temple is viewed as incorporating within itself such a spring, or as having been built upon the spring. The reason that such springs exist in temples is that they were perceived as the primeval waters of creation, *Nun* in Egypt, *abzu* in Mesopotamia, *tĕhôm* in Israel. The temple is thus founded upon and stands in contact with the waters of creation. These waters carry the dual symbolism of the chaotic waters that were organized during the creation and of the life-giving, saving nature of the waters of life.

4. The temple is built on separate, sacral, set-apart space.

5. The temple is associated with the tree of life.

6. The temple is oriented toward the four world regions or cardinal directions, and to various celestial bodies such as the polar star. As such, it is or can be an astronomical observatory, the main purpose of which is to assist the temple priests in regulating the ritual calendar. The earthly temple is also seen as a copy or counterpart of a heavenly model.

7. Temples, in their architectonic orientation, express the idea of a successive ascension toward heaven. The Mesopotamian ziggurat or staged temple tower is the best example of this architectural principle. It was constructed of three, five, or seven levels or stages. Monumental staircases led to the upper levels, where smaller temples stood. The basic ritual pattern represented in these

structures is that the worshippers ascended the staircase to the top, the deity descended from heaven, and the two met in the small temple which stood at the top of the structure.

8. The plan and measurements of the temple are revealed by God to the king or prophet, and the plan must be carefully carried out. The Babylonian king Nabopolassar stated that he took the measurements of Etemenanki, the temple tower in the main temple precinct at Babylon, under the guidance of the Babylonian gods Shamash, Adad, and Marduk, and that "he kept the measurements in his memory as a treasure."

9. The temple is the central, organizing, unifying institution in ancient Near Eastern society.

    a. The temple is associated with abundance and prosperity; indeed, it is perceived as the giver of these.

    b. The destruction or loss of the temple is seen as calamitous and fatal to the community in which the temple stood. The destruction is viewed as the result of social and moral decadence and disobedience to God's word.

10. Inside the temple, images of deities as well as living kings, temple priests, and worshippers are washed, anointed, clothed, fed, enthroned, and symbolically initiated into the presence of deity, and thus into eternal life. Further, New Year rites held in the temple include the reading and dramatic portrayal of texts which recite a pre-earthly war in heaven; a victory in that war by the forces of good, led by a chief deity; and the creation and establishment of the cosmos, cities, temples, and the social order. The sacred marriage is carried out at this time.

11. The temple is associated with the realm of the dead, the underworld, the afterlife, the grave. The unifying features here are the rites and worship of ancestors. Tombs can be, and in Egypt and elsewhere are, essentially temples (cf. the cosmic orientation, texts written on tomb walls which guide the deceased into the afterlife, etc.). The unifying principle between temple and tomb is resurrection. Tombs and sarcophagi are "sacred places," sites of resurrection. In Egyptian religion the sky goddess Nut is depicted on the coffin cover, symbolizing the cosmic orientation (cf. "Nut is the coffin."). The temple is the link between this world and the next.

12. Sacral, communal meals are carried out in connection with temple ritual, often at the conclusion of or during a covenant ceremony.

13. The tablets of destiny (or tablets of the decrees) are consulted in the cosmic sense by the gods, and yearly in a special temple chamber, *ubšukinna* in the temple of Eninnu in the time of the Sumerian king Gudea of Lagash. It was by this means that the will of deity was communicated to the people through the king or prophet for a given year.

14. God's word is revealed in the temple, usually in the holy of holies, to priests or prophets attached to the temple or to the religious system that it represents.

15. There is a close interrelationship between the temple and law in the ancient Near East. The building or restoration of a temple is perceived as the moving force behind a restating or "codifying" of basic legal principles, and of the "righting" and organizing of proper social order. The building or refurbishing of temples is central to the covenant process.

16. The temple is a place of sacrifice.

17. The temple and its ritual are enshrouded in secrecy. This secrecy relates to the sacredness of the temple precinct and the strict division in ancient times between sacred and profane space.

18. The temple and its cult are central to the economic structure of ancient Near Eastern society.[5]

The discussion that follows will sample passages in Isaiah that can be related to the temple typology outlined above, and does not claim to be an exhaustive study of the theme of the temple in Isaiah. The discussion will focus particularly on passages in Isaiah 2, 25, 28, and 30 that touch on the themes of cosmic mountain, communal meals in connection with covenant making, the relationship of the temple to the afterlife, the foundation stone of the temple in relation to the cosmic waters, the waters of life, and the centrality of the temple.

It was extremely commonplace among the ancient Near Eastern peoples to view temples as mountains. This comes out clearly in the terms applied to temples in the various traditions. For example, in Mesopotamia we find such temple names as "House of the Mountain" and "House of the Great Mountain of the Lands." Other temples are referred to as "The great house, it is a mountain great," "The house of Enlil, it is a mountain great," and so forth.[6] Ancient Sumerian inscriptions refer to a well-known temple as "a temple like a mountain in heaven and earth which raises its head to heaven," and note that "the temple, like a great mountain, is built up to heaven."[7] When I use the word "cosmic" in the phrase "cosmic mountain," this is simply to point out that the ancients assimilated temples to mountains where the divine presence was thought to have been manifest. As one scholar put it, the cosmic mountain was "a place set apart because of a divine presence or activity which relates to the world of man—ordering or stabilizing the world, acting upon it through natural forces, the point where the earth touches the divine sphere."[8]

This tradition is clearly evident in ancient Israel. In fact, notions of Mount Zion in Jerusalem, or the temple mount, as "the mountain of the Lord's house" that "shall be established in the top of the mountains" (Isaiah 2:2) go back ultimately to the experience at Sinai—*the* holy, cosmic mountain of scripture. The Temple of Solomon, built on the temple mount in Jerusalem, which was revealed to David by the Lord as the place where the temple should be built (see 2 Samuel 24), would seem to be basically the architectural realization and ritual enlargement of the Sinai experience.

Basic to temple ideology is the act of appearing "before the Lord," in Hebrew *liphnê Adonai*. As Menahem Haran states it: "In general, any cultic activity to which the biblical text applies the formula 'before the Lord' can be considered an indication of a temple at the site, since this expression stems from the basic conception of the temple as a divine dwelling place and actually belongs to the temple's technical terminology."[9] A more exact expression of the biblical view of the relationship between the phrase "before the Lord" and a cult installation has been given by Jacob Milgrom: "Does the expression 'before the Lord' imply only a temple or can it not apply equally to an open cult area? . . . Or rather should we not infer from the ancient law of Exodus 20:24 that God is present at the site of every theophany regardless of whether it is consecrated by the erection of a temple or an open altar?"[10] In any case, the "temple at the site" of the Sinai theophany is the mountain itself, and the events described in

Exodus 19-24 give us the perfect pattern for understanding what the temple experience was in ancient Israel, and indeed in much of the ancient Near Eastern world for that matter. This pattern involves ritual washings as part of the peoples' preparations to covenant themselves. It also involves the following sequence of events: the prophet ascends the mountain (read "temple") to meet with the Lord, and the Lord descends from his place in the heavens to meet with his prophet at the consecrated site; the prophet, after meeting personally with the Lord, returns to the people with the terms of the covenant as the Lord has expressed it to him; the people listen to the terms of the covenant and then assent to it with the characteristic biblical phrase, "All that the Lord hath spoken we will do" (Exodus 19:8). This is the semantic equivalent of the word "amen," the actual word used in Sumerian covenant ceremonies.[11] Following the delineation by the Lord of the definitions and terms of the covenant, the people have it read to them from a "book" by Moses, the only one who has actually appeared "before the Lord," to which they again assent: "All that the Lord hath said will we do, and be obedient." They are then sprinkled with the blood of a sacrificial animal, symbolic of the Savior, and enjoy a sacramental, covenantal meal together. (See Exodus 24:3-11.)

Thus when we read in Isaiah 2:2-3 (and in Micah 4:1-2) that the mountain of the Lord's house will be established in the tops of the mountains, and that all people will go up to it in order to learn of the God of Jacob and walk in his paths, this means that in the last days the temple of the Lord will be established (in the tops of the mountains), and that many people will have a desire to come into the temple of the Lord in order to learn of this covenant in order that they can covenant themselves to live his law. Thus we can be assured that virtually all scriptures which speak of the Lord's mountain are speaking of his temple. We must also remember here that the basic word for temple in both Sumerian and in Hebrew is "house," Sumerian é, which equals Akkadian bîtu and Hebrew *bayit*. Thus the temple is, in the poetic parallelism of the Hebrew Bible, the "mountain of the Lord" (Hebrew *har adonai*) and the "house of the God of Jacob" (Hebrew *bêt elōhê Yaqōb*).

Let us now turn to Isaiah 25:6-10. This passage, part of a much larger section commonly known as the "Apocalypse of Isaiah" (Isaiah 24-27), is contained within a chapter which speaks of the latter-day destruction of the proud and wicked, the rejoicing of the Saints, and the overcoming of death by the Lord. I will give verses 6 through 10 in two translations, the King James Version (KJV) and the New American Bible (NAB).

King James Version	New American Bible
6. And in this mountain shall the Lord of hosts make unto all people a feast of fat things, a feast of wines on the lees, of fat things full of marrow, of wines on the lees well refined.	6. On this mountain the Lord of hosts will provide for all peoples a feast of rich food and choice wines, juicy, rich food and pure, choice wines.
7. And he will destroy in this mountain the face of the covering cast over all people, and the vail that is spread over all nations.	7. On this mountain he will destroy the veil that veils all peoples, The web that is woven over all nations;
8. He will swallow up death in victory; and the Lord God will wipe away tears from off all faces; and the rebuke of his people shall he take away from off all the earth: for the Lord hath spoken it.	8. He will destroy death forever. The Lord God will wipe away the tears from all faces; The reproach of his people he will remove from the whole earth; for the Lord has spoken.
9. And it shall be said in that day, Lo, this is our God; we have waited for him, and he will save us: this is the Lord; we have waited for him, we will be glad and rejoice in his salvation.	9. On that day it will be said: "behold our God, to whom we looked to save us! This is the Lord for whom we looked; let us rejoice and be glad that he has saved us!"
10. For in this mountain shall the hand of the Lord rest, and Moab shall be trodden down under him, even as straw is trodden down for the dunghill.	10. For the hand of the Lord will rest on this mountain, but Moab will be trodden down as a straw is trodden down in the mire.

The key phrase here, of course, is "in (on) this mountain" in verses 6, 7, and 10. According to my interpretation outlined above, this phrase refers to the temple. To be sure, the sense of a millennial or messianic temple, such as we have in these passages, may be giving us a much wider view of the temple environs than we are used to in the historic Temple of Solomon. It may well be that in this and similar passages in Isaiah we are dealing not merely with the Jerusalem temple, but with Zion conceived as a *temple city,* which is the view of the latter-day temple that we get in Ezekiel (chapters 40-48) and in the Temple Scroll of the Qumran community. As Jacob Milgrom has written of the Qumran Temple Scroll's view of the latter-day temple, "The Temple city, requiring a three-day purification for admission, has the status of Mt. Sinai."[12] But we are still dealing with a view of Mount Zion, the temple, that incorporates and assimilates all the sanctity of Mount Sinai.

It is in the second part of verse 6 in the passage under discussion that we are drawn even more deeply into temple symbolism. In the NAB translation the whole verse reads, "On this mountain the Lord of hosts will provide for all people a feast of rich food and choice wines, juicy, rich food and pure, choice wines." We are dealing here with point number 12 of my typology above: "Sacral, communal meals are carried out in connection with temple ritual, often at the conclusion of or during a covenant ceremony." The evidence for such practices in ancient temple ritual is very widespread. The inscriptions of the ancient Sumerian king Gudea of the city of Lagash, who lived about 2100 B.C., record his building a temple to the chief deity of his city. The temple building itself resulted in an extraordinary abundance of the necessities of life, as pointed out in point 9 of the typology. Following the completion of the temple building, a great banquet was held at which the chief deities of the city, represented no doubt by their statues, were present. This banquet, at which the city's residents would no doubt have been present, was accompanied by a series of sacred vows or oaths sworn by the king, and by the determination of the city's destiny for the coming year.[13] From a much later period in history, the *akītu* or New Year's festival in Babylon—which celebrated the overcoming of evil forces in the premortal existence by Marduk, his creation of the earth, and the building of the temple in Babylon—was concluded "by a great sacrificial meal of which all the gods, the priests, and the people partook."[14]

The presence of a communal meal at the conclusion of a covenant ceremony, all within a temple context, is expressed very clearly in the Old Testament. The parade example of this point is the meal which "Moses, and Aaron, Nadab, and Abihu, and seventy of the elders of Israel" partook of with the Lord following the covenant ceremony that was sealed with the blood of the sacrificial animal (see Exodus 24:7-11). We find the same principle in the dedicatory prayer offered by Solomon at the completion of the building of the temple in Jerusalem. This prayer and the building of the temple, both of which clearly serve as symbols of the renewal of the covenant between the Lord and the Israelites which had existed for many centuries, were concluded with an enormous feast to which the entire congregation of Israel was invited. At the conclusion of the feast Solomon "sent the people away: and they blessed the king, and went unto their tents joyful and glad of heart for all the goodness that the Lord had done for David his servant, and for Israel his people." (See 1 Kings 8:62-66.)

The ultimate sacramental meal was the one celebrated in honor of the Savior, who "by his own blood . . . entered in once into the holy place, having obtained eternal redemption for us" (Hebrews 9:12). In this setting the temple imagery is very clear. Indeed, there is to be yet another messianic sacramental meal, and this too is spoken of in the scriptures within the context of the temple. We read in Revelation 19:9, "Blessed are they which are called unto the marriage supper of the Lamb." And earlier in the same book: "Therefore are they before the throne of God, and serve him day and night *in his temple:* and he that sitteth on the throne shall dwell among them. . . . For the Lamb which is in the midst of the throne *shall feed them,* and shall lead them unto living fountains of waters: and God shall wipe away all tears from their eyes." (Revelation 7:15, 17; emphasis added.) This same conjunction of concepts is found in the Doctrine and Covenants, where we read of "*a supper of the house of the Lord,* well prepared, unto which all nations shall be invited. . . . And after that cometh the day of my power; then shall the poor, the lame, and the blind, and the deaf, come in unto the *marriage of the Lamb, and partake of the supper of the Lord,* prepared for the great day to come" (D&C 58:9, 11; emphasis added). It is within this context of a millennial supper, to be enjoyed in the temple ("on this mountain") by all those who have entered into holy temple covenants with the Lord, that I believe the passage in Isaiah is to be understood.

This leads us to another of the many important themes of the passage in Isaiah 25. The theme in question is that of verse 8, "He will swallow up death in victory," and so on. In the typology outlined above, item number 11 states that "the temple is associated with the realm of the dead, the underworld, the afterlife, the grave." How does the "mountain" (i.e., the temple) overcome death? Or is it possible to see this passage within a temple context? I believe that it is. This is a rather complicated concept and will require a digression here to explain the relationship between temple and death, which I believe will at least partly illuminate this passage. A deeper examination of ancient Near Eastern temple rites will reveal an intimate relationship between the temple and the afterlife. A series of prehistoric temples at the site of Tepe Gawra in northern Iraq "attracted considerable numbers of burials to its precincts," according to the excavator.[15] In ancient Egypt, all temples were thought to have originated with the "primordial hillock," the first spot of ground to emerge after the waters of creation had subsided. According to Henri Frankfort, "Everywhere the site of creation, the first land to emerge from chaos, was thought to have been charged with vital power." And thus "each and every temple was supposed to stand on it."[16] The Egyptian pyramid, which itself carries all the architectural and religious overtones of a temple, also grew up out of the concept of the primordial mound. Frankfort says that "another architectural symbol for the Hill, the pyramid, was introduced in the Third Dynasty and modified in the Fourth. Djoser . . . realized the equation of his resting-place with the fountainhead of emerging life, the Primeval Hill, by giving his tomb the shape of a step pyramid, a three-dimensional form, as it were, of the hieroglyph for the Hill."[17]

Why was the connection made between the primordial hill of creation and a tomb? The answer, according to Frankfort, is that "the plot of ground from which creation proceeded was obviously a depository of creative energy powerful enough to carry anyone who might be buried there through the crisis of death to rebirth."[18] The same connection between temple and burial place is found in later Egyptian history, in the Edfu temples of Ptolemaic times. There, according to H. W. Fairman, "these Egyptian harvest festi-

speedily Osirianized and . . . they became funerary festivals. This also is markedly obvious at Edfu. The visit to the
Upper Temple was to a sacred necropolis, where were buried the
Divine Souls to whom offerings were made during the festival.
These Divine Souls were presumably the ancestral gods of Edfu.''
He tells us further that a series of texts at the temple describe how
the visits of Horus and Hathor ''brought these dead ancestral gods
life and light.''[19] Another scholar has written, ''It appears that
ceremonies for the ancestors were part of many, if not all, of the
great annual festivals; even more it seems reasonable also that
ceremonies for the (royal) ancestors formed part of the daily ritual
in all temples, and that they were celebrated immediately after the
conclusion of the daily ritual before the chief god.''[20]

There is a classic text in the aforementioned inscriptions of
Gudea, King of ancient Sumerian Lagash, that perhaps better than
any other gives expression to the central idea that connects the
temple with the afterlife. His inscriptions state that inside the
temple he built a chapel to the god Eninnu which was called ''the
house in which one brings offerings for the dead.'' This chapel
carried the further description ''it is something pure, purified by
Abzu.''[21] The ancient temple was seen as arising up out of the primordial waters of creation, *abzu* in Mesopotamia, *Nun* in Egypt,
tĕhôm in Israel. It rose out of these waters and ascended, as it
were, to heaven, thus incorporating the mountain symbolism
described above. Its foundations were sunk deeply in the abyss,
and its top reached into heaven. As such it constituted the central
pillar of the world, the place where all the main world regions—the
heavens, the earth, and the abyss or underworld—were united.
The temple was thought to have a *temen* or foundation serving as
its support and standing over the watery abyss, but with pillars
sunk deep into the foundations connecting it to the underworld.
One Sumerian text states that ''its [the temple's] foundation is
sunk deep into the Abyss.''[22] The same basic idea is expressed of
the Temple of Solomon, for example in Psalms 74 and 104 and in
Proverbs 8. In these passages, the mountains themselves constitute
the foundation of the earth.[23] The temple is thus thought of as the
''bond of heaven and earth,'' as the ''navel of the earth,'' and as
the ''pillar of the earth,'' that is, the central axis around which the
world revolves. The temple represents ''the Pole of the heavens,

around which all heavenly motions revolve, the knot that ties earth and heaven together, the seat of universal dominion.''[24]

Since ancient temples were thought to have been founded on the abyss, the primordial waters of creation, they were also thought both to control and to allow access to these same waters. Babylonian traditions indicate that the temple of Marduk in Babylon was founded upon and in the abyss (in Babylonian religion *abzu*, the abyss, is personified as the begetter of the human race, along with Tiamat). There are traditions in ancient texts which identify Babylon as the *bāb Apsī*, the "Gate of the Abyss," and indicate further that the temple at Babylon, the temple of Marduk, was seen as standing in a central position over the abyss, guarding access to these waters and subduing them.[25] Other texts indicate that each year, at the Babylonian New Year's festival, a ceremony was carried out in the *akītu* festival house in which either Marduk, the chief Babylonian god, or Bel, his son, was symbolically seated on top of a "sea," a cultic structure which represented Tiamat, the consort of Apsu. This symbolic action portrayed the victory of Marduk over the chaotic waters of creation, as recorded in the Babylonian epic of creation.[26]

We find the same symbolism applied to the Temple of Solomon in Jerusalem. Late Jewish traditions view Jerusalem as the center of the world, the highest point in the world, and the place where creation first was carried out. A famous Midrashic passage makes these points very clearly:

> Just as the navel is found at the center of a human being, so the land of Israel is found at the center of the world . . . and it is the foundation of the world. Jerusalem is at the center of the land of Israel, the Temple is at the center of Jerusalem, the Holy of Holies is at the center of the Temple, the ark is at the center of the Holy of Holies, and the Foundation Stone is in front of the ark, which spot is the foundation of the world.[27]

Jewish tradition sees the stone of foundation not only as the spot identifying the place where the world was created, but also sees it as marking the entry into the abyss, Hebrew *tĕhôm*. There is a Jewish tradition that God threw a stone into *tĕhôm*, thus making it the keystone of the earth and the foundation of the temple.[28] This gives us the view that the temple was founded on the first emerging earth after the waters of creation had receded, which is the same idea that we have in both Mesopotamia and Egypt. Burrows states that this legend "reminds one of the cosmogony of Eridu [the most ancient Sumerian city]—the first land and temple founded on the *abzu;* Palestinian stone takes the place of Mesopotamian reed-mat and earth."[29] A late Jewish Targum states that the stone of foundation in the temple "closes the mouth of the *tĕhôm*," This would make of the rock a kind of *bāb Apsî,* "gate of the abyss," such as was described in relation to Babylon above.[30] It is important to note that, in all the ancient traditions I have been discussing, the underground waters of creation bear a dual and ambiguous symbolism. They are the disorderly waters of chaos that were controlled by God during the creative process, and thus are seen as forces hostile to God, but they also bear the overtones of life, the source of life and the source of the sweet waters that make life possible. The theme of the Lord's overcoming the hostile waters is very widely expressed in the Old Testament, as for example in Psalms 29:10; 74:12-15; 93:1-5; and 104:5-9.

Ancient texts give us a vivid impression of the creative, positive forces that were thought to be associated with the underground waters. In ancient Sumer, the god of the ancient temple in Eridu was Enki, the god of the abyss, considered to be a god of wisdom. The inscriptions of Gudea of Lagash state that it was Enki who taught Gudea the plan of the temple that he was to build.[31] Another passage in these inscriptions states that he built the holy of holies of this temple "like the abyss in a pure place."[32] These same inscriptions indicate the belief that the waters of abundance that are brought forth as a result of the building of the temple come forth from deep springs within the earth.[33] In ancient Egypt, but from a much later period than that of Gudea, we find a similar phenomenon. Through the course of Egyptian history, measuring devices (called Nilometers by scholars) were built along the shores of the Nile, with the ostensible purpose of measuring the height of the Nile. But there is much more to their function. A lengthy quotation from a recent work will serve to describe their religious functions:

> Although Nilometers were primarily designed to measure the Nile flood, they also served as sources of water. Because virtually all known Nilometers have an evident connection with a sanctuary, H. W. Fairman suggested that they were intended to provide pure Nile water for liturgical rites and were not utilized

for more ordinary needs. Several factors offer support for this viewpoint. First of all, because the entrances to these Nilometers are usually situated inside the precinct, these installations in effect served to bring the Nile within the sacred area. Secondly, at Edfu and apparently also at the Temple of Amun at Karnak, the Nilometer is situated directly to the right of the central adytum, a location perhaps intended to underscore the importance of this facility for the sacred rites. A most significant factor is the relationship of these Nilometers to the Nile flood. While Egyptians considered water drawn from the Nile during any season to be sacred, it enjoyed this character only by extension. The sacred Nile water *par excellence* was the water of the annual inundation [and thus the waters of Nun]. The flood represented a "renewal" or even a "rebirth" of the river; as early as the Old Kingdom its waters were called "the new water."[34]

Here we see that the Nile waters, thought by the ancient Egyptians to represent the primordial waters of Nun, were thought to be so important that they were channeled into the holy of holies of the temple in order to be more directly available for ritual purposes. We can also document the importance of the deep underground waters as sources of life in the Old Testament. In the well-known passage in Jeremiah 2:13, the Lord is referred to as "the fountain of living waters," which the Israelites have rejected in favor of "broken cisterns, that can hold no water." Verse 18 of the same chapter contains taunting references to the futility of drinking the waters of the Nile or of the Euphrates River, and is probably a sarcastic reference by the prophet to the very views held by the Mesopotamians and Egyptians about the *abzu* and the *Nun*, outlined above. He is saying, in other words, that the waters of the *abzu* and the *Nun* have no saving value, in spite of the elaborate mythologies that have been developed around them and their saving qualities. Only the waters that come from the deep source of life itself, the Lord, have saving value. The Hebrew word used here for "fountain" is *māqôr,* which is a deep well or spring, arising from the subterranean water sources. A passage similar to the one in Jeremiah 2:13 is found in Psalm 36:8-9 (vss. 9-10 in the Hebrew). Verse 9 reads: "For with thee is the fountain of life: in thy light shall we see light." The Hebrew word for "fountain" here is the same as in Jeremiah. The "fountain of life" in Psalm 36:9 comes from the Hebrew *mĕqôr hayyîm.* The same idea is

found in Numbers 19:17, *mayîm ḥayyîm,* "living waters," translated as "running water" in the KJV. It is this idea that underlies
the Savior's statement to the Samaritan woman at the well in John
4:10. The "living waters" are the sweet, flowing waters that come
to the surface as springs that originated deep underground. This is
the only water that was allowed for many ritual observances under
the Mosaic law, such as the ritual of the red heifer of Numbers
19.[35]

To return, then, to the question that occasioned this long
digression: how is death overcome "on this mountain"? What
symbolism underlies the ancient view that death is overcome in the
temple? Dr. Nibley has written that "many studies have demonstrated the identity of tomb, temple, and palace as the place where
the powers of the other world are exercised for the benefit of the
human race."[36] The temple controls access to the three world
regions, the heavens, the earth, and the underworld. As such it
serves as the gate to the underworld, the place that represents both
life and death. And the Lord is the master of these powers. We
read in the NAB text of Psalm 29:9-10:

> 9. The voice of the Lord twists the oaks and strips the for-
> ests, and in his temple all say, "Glory!"
> 10. The Lord is enthroned above the flood; the Lord is en-
> throned as king forever.

Perhaps the clearest biblical expression of the relationship between
the temple, the Lord, and the overcoming of death is found in a
passage in Revelation where Isaiah 25:8 is quoted. The most
interesting thing about this passage is its reference to the "living
fountains of waters," which as we have seen above are everywhere
connected with the life-giving powers of the temple. The passage is
Revelation 7:15-17, which reads in the KJV:

> 15. Therefore are they before the throne of God, and serve
> him day and night *in his temple:* and he that sitteth on the
> throne shall dwell among them.
> 16. They shall hunger no more, neither thirst any more;
> neither shall the sun light on them, nor any heat.
> 17. For the Lamb which is in the midst of the throne shall
> feed them, and shall *lead them unto living fountains of waters:*
> and God *shall wipe away all tears from their eyes.* (Emphasis
> added.)

To give a general summary of our discussion of the passage in Isaiah 25:6-8, a quotation from Frank Moore Cross seems relevant: "At the feast on the mountain, Death (Mot) was to be 'swallowed up' forever."[37]

The next passage in Isaiah that I would like to discuss is found in chapter 28, verses 14 to 18. In the NAB these verses read:

14. Therefore, hear the word of the Lord, you arrogant, who rule this people in Jerusalem:
15. Because you say, "We have made a covenant with death, and with the nether world we have made a pact; When the overwhelming scourge passes, it will not reach us; For we have made lies our refuge, and in falsehood we have found a hiding place,"
16. Therefore, thus says the Lord God: See, I am laying a stone in Zion, a stone that has been tested, A precious corner-stone as a sure foundation; he who puts his faith in it shall not be shaken.
17. I will make of right a measuring line, of justice a level. Hail shall sweep away the refuge of lies, and waters shall flood the hiding place.
18. Your covenant with death shall be cancelled and your pact with the nether world shall not stand. When the over-whelming scourge passes, you shall be trampled down by it.

These verses contain important themes from the symbolism of the ancient temple that have been discussed above: the rock of foundation in Zion—that is, the temple Holy of Holies in Jerusalem, from where creation was thought to have been begun—and the chaotic, destructive waters of the abyss. We are introduced in verse 15 to two subdivisions of the biblical abyss, *tĕhôm*, namely "death" (Hebrew *māvet*) and the "nether world" (Hebrew *shĕôl*). As explained above, the temple brings these underworld regions into contact with the heavenly spheres. According to A. J. Wensinck, "The sanctuary is not only the center of the earth, it possesses also another characteristic of the navel, namely that of being the place of communication with the upper and with the nether world, or, on the one hand with heaven in general and with Paradise and the divine throne in particular—on the other hand with Tehom in general and with the realm of the dead and Hell in particular; in other words: in the sanctuary the three parts of the Universe, earth, upper and nether world meet."[38] Verse 16 of this passage depicts the stone of foundation as the "usual Oriental theme of the sacred foundation upon the gate of the *apsu* or mouth of the *těhôm* or entrance to the underworld."[39] A group of evil people is depicted as having made a covenant with "death" and the "nether world," thinking that they can avoid being swept away by the destructive waters of the abyss. But it is only in the "stone in Zion," the "precious cornerstone as a sure foundation," that there is to be true salvation from the onrushing waters of the abyss. It is the Stone of Foundation that controls access to the abyss, and only through this stone that the destructive waters can be controlled. Any kind of pact or covenant made with the abyss that seeks to avoid entering in at the only true "gate of the abyss" will end in destruction. The temple is the place of salvation, and the Savior is the Lord of the temple, and the only gate which will "cancel the covenant with death and with the nether world" and help those who "put faith in it" (that is, the cornerstone) to avoid the "overwhelming scourge." He also is the "stone in Zion" (see Romans 9:33; 1 Peter 2:6-8).

This passage also has great significance in the interpretation of Matthew 16:13-19. According to Eric Burrows, "That there is allusion to the rock of the temple (in Matt. 16:18) is made practically certain by the evident parallelism between the passage in the gospel and an oracle of Isaiah (28:16)." In Matthew 16:18, the Savior declares that his church is built on "this rock," and that the "gates of hell," literally "gates of Hades," where Hades is equivalent to Hebrew *shěôl,* shall not prevail against it. Burrows further states that "all is explained if the allusion is to the Stone of Foundation firmly established over *shěôl* and the *těhôm.*"[40] He also speculates on the evidence given in Matthew and Mark that may enable us to date the occasion of the Savior's words to Peter concerning the rock. The evidence makes it possible to conclude that these words were spoken on the Day of Atonement, that day in Israelite life when the sanctity of the temple was brought most to the forefront. It would indeed have been appropriate for the Savior to make a speech on that day that was so profoundly rooted in the symbolism of the temple.[41]

I would next like to discuss an isolated passage from a larger oracle that deals with the latter-day prosperity and abundance of Zion. The passage in question relates to point number 3 of the typology above, where it is stated that "the temple is often associated with the waters of life which flow from a spring within the building itself." This verse, Isaiah 30:25, will help to extend our understanding of how the temple was viewed by the ancient peoples of the Middle East. This verse reads in the NAB: "Upon every high mountain and lofty hill there will be streams of running water." The temple is a symbol of abundance and prosperity, as pointed out above, and this abundance is symbolized by a stream of water that issues forth from under the temple itself. As Dr. Nibley has written: "At every hierocentric shrine stood a mountain or artificial mound and a lake or spring from which four streams flowed out to þring the life-giving waters to the four regions of the earth. The place was a green paradise, a carefully kept garden, a refuge from drought and heat. Elaborate waterworks figure conspicuously in the appointments and the rites of the holy place."[42] This is actually a good description of the larger oracle from which I have extracted the single verse. Verses 23 to 26 describe a millennial paradise, well watered and well fed with luxuriant vegetation abounding. In the middle of this paradise will stand temples, each with a stream of water flowing from underneath the foundations. According to Wensinck, "Springs generally rise on the mountains; and a spring, with or without a mountain, is, generally speaking, a necessary requisite in a sanctuary." Wensinck gives evidence from Jewish and Muslim traditions to show that Jerusalem was thought of as "being the origin of all sweet water on the earth." An early Muslim writer, Abu Huraira, speaking on the authority of the prophet Muhammad, said that "all rivers and clouds and vapours and winds come from under the holy rock in Jerusalem."[43]

These waters represent the positive aspects of the abyss, the clear, deep, fast-moving and pure waters that represent the source of life. In the Ugaritic myths from Ras Shamra, one section of the so-called Baal Cycle speaks of the location of the dwelling place of El, the father of Baal. In the translation of Richard Clifford this passage reads:

Then they set face
Toward El at the sources of the Two Rivers,
In the midst of the pools of the Double Deep.
They entered the tent of El and went into
The tent shrine of the king, the father of years.[44]

We have already seen above what role the Nile waters played in the ritual of Egyptian temples. H. W. Fairman reports that the libation water used in the daily service in Edfu temples was taken from a well dug underneath the east side of the temple, just outside the holy of holies. This meant that the waters in a sacred lake situated nearby, but not in direct access to the holy of holies, were not sufficiently pure for the ritual usages. The water had to be located in or near the holy of holies itself, and to flow from underneath the temple.[45]

There are a number of passages in the Old and New Testaments that speak of springs of water issuing from underneath the temple of the Lord. The passages are Joel 3:18; Ezekiel 47:1; Zechariah 14:8 ("living waters shall go out from Jerusalem"); and Revelation 22:1 ("a pure river of water of life, clear as crystal, proceeding out of the throne of God and of the Lamb"). All of these passages are millennial in time reference, with the exception of the passage in Revelation, which seems to be celestial in reference. The Prophet Joseph Smith spoke in a similar vein, stating that "Jerusalem must be rebuilt.—& Judah return, must return & the temple water come out from under the temple—the waters of the dead sea be healed . . . & all this must be done before Son of Man will make his appearance [sic]."[46] The theme of "messianic water" is very strongly emphasized within the context of a covenantal meal in Isaiah 55:1-3.

Thus I have attempted to demonstrate how profoundly the book of Isaiah, and indeed the Bible in general, is permeated with temple symbolism. The few passages that I have discussed represent a mere fragment of such symbolism in Isaiah. A full study of this subject would require a large volume. Great benefits can come from such study, showing us as it does how central the temple was in all the cultures of the ancient Near East. Jonathan Z. Smith, quoting a commentary from *Mishnah Abot* on the well-known dictum "on three things the world stands: on the law, on the temple service, and on piety," adds the comment: "The temple and its ritual serve as the cosmic pillars or the 'sacred pole' supporting the world. If its service is interrupted or broken, if an error is made, then the world, the blessing, the fertility, indeed all of creation which flows from the Center, will likewise be disrupted."[47] Perhaps an appropriate closing quotation could come from another temple-centered passage in the NAB text of Isaiah 56:7:

Them I will bring to my holy mountain and make joyful in my house of prayer; Their holocausts and sacrifices will be acceptable on my altar, For my house shall be called a house of prayer for all peoples.

Notes

1. Martyrdom of Isaiah 3-5, in R. H. Charles, ed., *The Pseudepigrapha*, vol. 2 of *The Apocrypha and Pseudepigrapha of the Old Testament* (Oxford: Clarendon Press, 1913), pp. 161-62.

2. A. R. Johnson, *Sacral Kingship in Ancient Israel* (Cardiff: University of Wales Press, 1967), pp. 13-14.

3. Folker Willesen, "The Cultic Situation of Psalm LXXIV," *Vetus Testamentum 2* (1952):290.

4. Hugh W. Nibley, *What Is a Temple? The Idea of the Temple in History* (Provo: Brigham Young University Press, 1963), pp. 8-9.

5. The preceding typology is a revision of the list included in John M. Lundquist, "What Is a Temple? A Preliminary Typology," in *The Quest for the Kingdom of God: Studies in Honor of George E. Mendenhall* (Winona Lake, Ind.: Eisenbrauns, 1982).

6. For references see ibid.

7. F. Thureau-Dangin, *Die Sumerischen und Akkadischen Königsinschriften* (Leipzig: J. C. Hinrichs, 1907), pp. 23, 13.

8. Richard Clifford, *The Cosmic Mountain in Canaan and in the Old Testament* (Cambridge: Harvard University Press, 1972), pp. 7-8.

9. Menahem Haran, *Temples and Temple Service in Ancient Israel* (Oxford: Clarendon Press, 1978), p. 26.

10. Jacob Milgrom, "Review of Temples and Temple Service in Ancient Israel," *Journal of the American Oriental Society* 101 (1981):262.

11. The Sumerian term is *heam*, "let it be." See Thorkild Jacobsen, *Toward the Image of Tammuz and Other Essays on Mesopotamian History and Culture*, ed. William L. Moran (Cambridge: Harvard University Press, 1970), p. 138.

12. Jacob Milgrom, "The Temple Scroll," *Biblical Archeologist* 41 (1978):114.

13. Adam Falkenstein, *Die Inschriften Gudeas von Lagash*, vol. 30 of *Analecta Orientalia* (Rome: Pontificium Institutum Biblicum, 1966), p. 120.

14. Svend Aage Pallis, *The Babylonian Akitu Festival* (Copenhagen: Bianco Lunos Bogtrykkeri, 1926), p. 173.

15. Arthur J. Tobler, *Excavations at Tepe Gawra,* Museum Monographs (Philadelphia: University of Pennsylvania Press, 1950), 2:98-101.

16. Henri Frankfort, *Kingship and the Gods* (Chicago: University of Chicago Press, 1948), pp. 151-52.

17. Ibid.

18. Ibid.

19. H. W. Fairman, "Worship and Festivals in an Egyptian Temple," *Bulletin of the John Rylands Library* 37 (1954-55):200.

20. Mohiy elDin Ibrahim, "The God of the Great Temple of Edfu," in *Glimpses of Ancient Egypt: Studies in Honor of H. W. Fairman,* ed. John Ruffle et al., Orbis Aegyptiorum Speculum (Warminster: Aris & Phillips, 1979), p. 171.

21. Falkenstein, *Die Inschriften Gudeas von Lagash,* p. 131.

22. A. Falkenstein, "Sumerische Bauausdrücke," *Orientalia* 35 (1966):236.

23. A. J. Wensinck, *The Ideas of the Western Semites Concerning the Navel of the Earth* (Amsterdam: Johannes Muller, 1916), pp. 2-4.

24. A. Jeremias, quoted in Nibley, *What Is a Temple?* p. 3.

25. Eric Burrows, "Some Cosmological Patterns in Babylonian Religion," in *The Labyrinth,* ed. S. H. Hooke (London: Society for Promoting Christian Knowledge, 1935), p. 50.

26. W. G. Lambert, "The Great Battle of the Mesopotamian Religious Year: The Conflict in the Akitu House," *Iraq* 25 (1963):189-90.

27. Midrash Tanhuma, Kedoshim 10, quoted in Jonathan Z. Smith, *Map Is Not Territory,* vol. 23 of *Studies in Judaism in Late Antiquity* (Leiden: E. J. Brill, 1978), p. 112.

28. Burrows, "Some Cosmological Patterns," p. 55.

29. Ibid.

30. Ibid.

31. Thureau-Dangin, *Die Sumerischen und Akkadischen Königsinschriften,* pp. 108-9.

32. Ibid., pp. 116-17.

33. Ibid., pp. 104-5.

34. Robert A. Wild, *Water in the Cultic Worship of Isis and Sarapis,* vol. 87 of *Etudes Prelim. aux Religions Orient. dans l'Empire Romain* (Leiden: E. J. Brill, 1981), pp. 27-28.

35. Hermann L. Strack and Paul Billerbeck, *Das Evangelium nach Markus, Lukas und Johannes und die Apostelgeschichte,* vol. 2 of *Kommentar zum*

Neuen Testament aus Talmud und Midrasch (Munich: C. H. Beck, 1924), p. 436.

36. Nibley, *What Is a Temple?* p. 5.

37. Frank Moore Cross, Jr., *Canaanite Myth and Hebrew Epic* (Cambridge: Harvard University Press, 1973), p. 144.

38. A. J. Wensinck, *The Navel of the Earth* (Amsterdam: Johannes Muller, 1916), p. 23.

39. Burrows, "Some Cosmological Patterns," p. 58.

40. Ibid., pp. 58-59.

41. Ibid.

42. Hugh W. Nibley, "The Hierocentric State," *Western Political Quarterly* 4 (1951):235.

43. Wensinck, *The Navel of the Earth*, pp. 30, 33-34.

44. Richard Clifford, "The Temple in the Ugaritic Myth of Baal," in *Symposia*, ed. Frank M. Cross (Cambridge: American Schools of Oriental Research, 1979), p. 145.

45. Fairman, "Worship and Festivals in an Egyptian Temple," pp. 177-78.

46. *The Words of Joseph Smith*, comp. and ed. Andrew F. Ehat and Lyndon W. Cook (Provo, Utah: Religious Studies Center, Brigham Young University, 1980), p. 180.

47. Smith, *Map Is Not Territory*, p. 118.

3

The Marriage of Hosea and Jehovah's Covenant with Israel

Kent P. Jackson

The ministry of the prophet Hosea is generally placed in the turbulent third quarter of the eighth century B.C. Approximately two centuries earlier, the great Israelite empire of David and Solomon had divided into two rival nations, Israel in the north and Judah in the south. Hosea's stewardship was primarily to the Northern Kingdom. His ministry began during the reign of Jeroboam II, when both kingdoms were prosperous and wealthy. The two great powers of the day, Egypt and Assyria, were then less involved in Syria-Palestine than at other times. As a result, the smaller kingdoms, which during other periods had fallen into their respective spheres of influence, now were able to concentrate on internal and external affairs to their own benefit. Jeroboam's reign was characterized by growth and consolidation. Yet the wealth of the two kingdoms in Palestine was not that of nations blessed with the riches of righteousness; their prosperity was not that of those who serve the Lord. Indeed, the prophets denounced both nations for their wickedness. Amos, a contemporary of Hosea, decried Israel's oppression of the poor and the excesses of the rich. Hosea announced God's severance of his covenant relationship with Israel. Both foretold the bitter consequence of that action.

That consequence was soon forthcoming. Hosea undoubtedly witnessed many of the tragic events that culminated in the destruction of his nation. Within a few years of the beginning of his ministry, the Assyrian Empire began extending its influence into Palestine. Soon both Israel and Judah were subjected to Assyrian vassalage. In Israel that status was not to be permanent, for during the reign of King Hoshea, records the biblical writer, "the king of Assyria found conspiracy" in Israel (2 Kings 17:4).[1] "Then the king of Assyria came up throughout all the land, and went up to Samaria, and besieged it three years. In the ninth year of Hoshea the king of Assyria took Samaria, and carried Israel away into Assyria" (2 Kings 17:5-6).

The utter horror of a three-year siege followed by capture and deportation is part of the fulfillment of prophecy. The house of Israel had been warned that the breach of covenants made with God would bring sure calamity, including destruction and scattering (e.g., see Deuteronomy 4:25-27). Hosea, possibly more than any other prophet, proclaimed publicly that God had canceled that covenant, that the divine protection afforded by it would no longer exist, and that the punishment resulting from its violation would soon be realized. He delivered his message to Israel in the generation immediately prior to their destruction. It is no wonder, then, that his preaching takes for granted the inevitability of that event.

The Marriage

Undoubtedly the most noteworthy issue in the writings of the prophet Hosea, at least from a Latter-day Saint perspective, is the strange account of his marriage, by divine command, to an immoral woman: "And the Lord said to Hosea, Go, take unto thee a wife of whoredoms" (Hosea 1:2). To Latter-day Saint readers, who understand the nature and role of prophets, it seems surprising—if not shocking—that God would command his prophet to marry a woman described in these terms; elsewhere she is called an adultress (Hosea 3:1). Since ancient times, commentators have debated whether this divinely arranged marriage actually took place or whether it was only figurative, as an allegory of God's relationship to Israel. Since the essential points of the many interpretations of this issue can be found elsewhere, only a summary follows.[2] Briefly stated, the three main lines of interpretation are as follows: (1) The marriage described refers to the actual condition of Hosea's marrying, by a commandment of God, a promiscuous, immoral woman. This interpretation takes the account literally as recorded. (2) Possibly the woman was not immoral when Hosea married her but became so later. In this case Hosea 1:2 mistakenly records that she was originally "a wife of whoredoms," or possibly it anticipates her later behavior. (3) The entire account is an allegory of Jehovah's relationship to Israel, an immoral and promiscuous nation, and does not record an actual historical circumstance.

My inclination is to reject number one, the literal interpretation. I believe there may be merit in either number two or number three.

The main issue in Hosea's prophecy is *not* his relationship with his wife but God's relationship with Israel. When God established that relationship, Israel was pure. It was not until later that Israel apostatized and violated the covenant. Yet in a distant day, following the rejection, separation, and punishment resulting from that breach of covenant, Israel would repent and Jehovah would bring her back and establish the covenant anew. Hosea's domestic situation may have followed the same pattern. Perhaps he was married to a woman of integrity who afterwards became an adultress. After her immoral escapades and the punishment and separation that resulted from them, she may have repented and returned to Hosea, her long-suffering husband, who then took her back forgivingly and renewed his vows with her. What better object lesson than his own marital history could Hosea have used to teach the principles that underscore the covenant history of God and Israel? One can almost hear Hosea proclaiming on the streets of Samaria: "Look at us! Just as you are unfaithful to Jehovah, my wife was unfaithful to me. Just as she had to bear the consequences of her infidelity, so must you. But just as she has repented and returned and I have welcomed her back, so must you do away with false gods, repent, and return to Jehovah. And he will take you back also." This interpretation seems more likely to me than does the one in which God literally commands his prophet to marry someone who already is a woman "of whoredoms" and "an adultress."

The third possibility to which I have referred assumes that the account is not to be taken literally at all but simply seen as an allegory employed by Hosea to illustrate the relationship that existed between God and Israel. The "unfaithful wife" metaphor is used elsewhere in the Hebrew Bible to describe that relationship, but it is only in Hosea that it is expressed by means of the domestic circumstances of a prophet.

As stated already, the message of the book is not Hosea's family life, but rather the relationship between God and his people. Hosea's marriage and the names of his children are the vehicles by which the real message is conveyed. That is clear from the two parallel passages in which the prophet is commanded to take his wife: "And the Lord said to Hosea, Go, take unto thee a wife of whoredoms and children of whoredoms: *for the land hath committed great whoredom, departing from the Lord*" (Hosea 1:2); and "Go yet, love a woman beloved of her friend, yet an adultress, *according to the love of the Lord toward the children of Israel, who look to other gods*" (Hosea 3:1). In both cases we are told that the purpose of Hosea's marriage, as far as the prophecy is concerned, is to exemplify Jehovah's ruined relationship with Israel. Whether we assume that an actual marriage of Hosea was involved or not is irrelevant to the purposes of the book; either way the greater message comes through. The message itself, however, was of vital importance to the house of Israel in Hosea's time, and its relevance has not diminished over the twenty-seven centuries since then. What better way could there be to teach that message than through the analogy of marriage?

When a man and a woman enter into the sacred covenant of marriage, they make certain promises to each other, either explicitly or implicitly, which form the very foundation of their union. Chief among these covenant promises are honesty, unfailing love, and strict faithfulness. Often in the scriptures the covenant which God made with Israel is referred to as a marriage covenant. The same conditions which are at the core of the bond of marriage are also at the core of the bond between Jehovah and Israel—honesty, love, and fidelity. The covenant of marriage and God's covenant with his chosen people are, in fact, very similar. Hosea's message concerning Jehovah and his people is expressed in that kind of language. Yet even more graphically, the violation of that covenant of honesty, love, and fidelity is expressed as adultery—the violation of the sanctity of marriage. The dissolution of that covenant is described as divorce.

According to the biblical account, Hosea's marriage to Gomer, daughter of Diblaim, resulted in the births of three children who had symbolic names. The first was a son, Jezreel, "for yet a little while, and I will avenge the blood of Jezreel upon the house of Jehu, and will cause to cease the kingdom of the house of Israel" (Hosea 1:4). Conveyed in this symbolic name is a forewarning of the Lord's vengeance on Jehu's dynasty and the destruction of the kingdom of Israel. Jehu was the king who had come to power in Israel by overthrowing the previous king in the city of Jezreel, beginning his massacre of the descendants of King Ahab. Jehu's descendants still ruled Israel in Hosea's day. The use of the name Jezreel is a prophetic pronouncement that the blood shed by Jehu at that place would now be avenged upon his dynasty, whose kings were wicked like their ancestor.

The second child, a daughter, is introduced in verse 6. Hosea was commanded to call her "Lo-ruhama: for I will no more have mercy upon the house of Israel; but I will utterly take them away." The name *lō' rūḥāmâ* means "not pitied" or "not having obtained compassion," and its prophetic message is, "I will no more have mercy [more accurately translated 'pity' or 'compassion'] upon the house of Israel; but I will utterly take them away"—no more pity, no more compassion.

The third child, a son, was given a name of similar meaning: "Then said God, Call his name Lo-ammi: for ye are not my people, and I will not be your God" (Hosea 1:9). The name *lō' 'ammî* means simply "not my people." Its message is clear: Israel is no longer God's people, and he is no longer Israel's God.

To understand the full impact of God's announcement that he was terminating the covenant relationship which he had with Israel, we must go back to that great event when the covenant was established at Sinai. Even prior to that, however, the Lord announced to the patriarchs his choosing of their future seed. And through Moses, before the deliverance of Israel from Egypt, the Lord proclaimed, "And I will take you to me for a people, and I will be to you a God" (Exodus 6:7). When the actual covenant was established between God and Israel at Sinai, the Lord announced, "If ye will obey my voice indeed, and keep my covenant, then ye shall be a peculiar treasure unto me above all people" (Exodus 19:5). A better translation of "a peculiar treasure unto me" would be "my special possession" or "my treasured property." This is a unique relationship. It is a relationship of love and commitment, a treasured status not available to all the world but reserved for the house of Israel. The cancellation of that relationship, as announced by Hosea, is one of the greatest tragedies in human history, a tragedy that continues to have profound implications in our time, not only theologically but politically as well.

In chapter 2, Hosea shifts his emphasis to the unfaithful and immoral character of his wife. He announces in verse 2 that "she is not my wife, neither am I her husband." This is essentially an announcement of divorce; Jehovah has divorced Israel. What begins now is bitter condemnation of Israel's behavior and a proclamation that God would punish her severely for it. He would publicly expose his unfaithful wife to ridicule, shame, and abuse because she violated her vows to him. He would expose her adultery to the world and humiliate her before her lovers: "Let her therefore put away her whoredoms out of her sight, and her adulteries from between her breasts; lest I strip her naked, and set her as in the day that she was born, and make her as a wilderness. . . . I will discover her lewdness in the sight of her lovers, and none shall deliver her out of mine hand" (Hosea 2:2-3, 10). In verse 12 the Lord vows to destroy the productivity of the land, which promiscuous Israel attributes to her lovers, saying "these are my rewards that my lovers have given me." In Canaanite religion, the productivity of land and cattle is assured through worship of the deified forces of nature. The Israelites were involved in this type of worship and were therefore denounced forcefully by the Old Testament prophets. Hosea here accuses Israel, Jehovah's unfaithful spouse, of having illicit intercourse with the Baals, exchanging sexual favors for the good things of the earth, blessings that come only from the true husband, Jehovah. The Lord promises to annihilate the productivity of the earth and turn back Israel's vines and fig trees to pristine forest, food for "the beasts of the field."

God's condemnation of his adulterous consort is the punishment that she must receive for her infidelity. Other prophets foretold even more graphically than did Hosea the extent to which Israel would be punished for her sins following her rejection by the Lord. The picture painted in the scriptures of the years of separation from the covenant blessings is not a happy one. Through Ezekiel, for example, the Lord proclaimed that he would consume

Israel in the furnace of his fury: "Yea, I will gather you, and blow upon you in the fire of my wrath, and ye shall be melted in the midst thereof. As silver is melted in the midst of the furnace, so shall ye be melted in the midst thereof; and ye shall know that I the Lord have poured out my fury upon you." (Ezekiel 22:21-22.)

Though the separation is deserved and the punishment sure and inevitable, neither is irreversible. The Lord has vowed to make available to Israel, following her purging and repentance, "a door of hope" (Hosea 2:15), something that a modern-day prophet has called a "miracle of forgiveness."[3] After the punishment and repentance are complete, the Lord will take her back. As Hosea describes it, that reunion would be characterized by Israel's referring to Jehovah as "Ishi" (Hosea 2:16), "my husband," and not as "Baali," which also means "my husband" but means as well "my Baal." In other words, Israel would then know to whom indeed she had a covenant obligation and would be faithful to that bond.

Since Jehovah has divorced Israel, the renewal of covenant is described as a reestablishment of the marriage: "And I will betroth thee unto me for ever; yea, I will betroth thee unto me in righteousness, and in judgment, and in lovingkindness, and in mercies. I will even betroth thee unto me in faithfulness: and thou shalt know the Lord." (Hosea 2:19-20.) This describes the permanent reunion of the repentant wife to the ever-forgiving husband. Notice some of the key words: "lovingkindness," "faithfulness," and "thou shalt know the Lord." The reestablishment of the covenant is finalized in verse 23: "And I will sow her unto me in the earth; and I will have mercy upon her that had not obtained mercy; and I will say to them which were not my people, Thou art my people; and they shall say, Thou art my God." An English translation cannot convey the beauty and skill of the Hebrew text. Hosea's wordplay here is superb as he uses the names of the three children, not to express the dissolution of the covenant as he did in chapter 1, but to show its renewal. The name of the first child, Jezreel, means "God sows" or "God will sow." It is used in this verse to depict the restoration of Israel in the land: "I will sow her unto me in the earth." The name of the second child follows: "I will have compassion upon *lō' rūḥāmâ*," or "I will have compassion upon her that had not obtained compassion." And finally, "I will say to lō-'ammî, 'ammî-'atâ." or "to not my people, 'you are my people,' and he shall say, 'you are my God.' " The precious relationship which is described in so many places in the scriptures as the core of God's dealings with Israel is now restored once again: "You are my people, and I am your God."

Hosea was not alone in using these words to describe the reestablishment of the covenant relationship between Jehovah and his people. As we saw already in Exodus 6, the Lord used them with regard to establishing this covenant relationship in the first place. In Ezekiel, following a description of cleansing, spiritual renewal, and reestablishment of covenant, the Lord says, "And ye shall dwell in the land that I gave to your fathers; and ye shall be my people, and I will be your God" (Ezekiel 36:28). In the next chapter Ezekiel highlights repentance and cleansing in recording his millennial message: "So shall they be my people, and I will be their God" (Ezekiel 37:23). Later in the same chapter, in a passage referring to the millennial reign of the Savior, which follows Israel's acceptance of an "everlasting covenant," we read, "I will be their God, and they shall be my people" (Ezekiel 37:27). In all of these passages it is clear that this special status exists only when the covenant is intact, contingent upon the faithfulness and obedience of the people. When the stipulations of the covenant are not met, it is not in force, and God rightly states, "You are not my people, and I am not your God"—or, using the marriage metaphor with reference to Israel, "She is not my wife, neither am I her husband" (Hosea 2:2). And so the situation must remain until Israel, the covenant-breaking party, repents.

Hosea chapter 3 presents the same story of Hosea and his wife, but with different details and additional information. Some scholars argue that this chapter introduces a second wife; but that, in my view, is unlikely, though admittedly the relationship between the two accounts is problematic.[4] The narrative in chapter 3 is in the first person, while that in chapters 1 and 2 is in third person. Of significance for the chapter 3 account is the fact that Hosea buys his wife for a price. Much scholarly discussion has been generated over the issue of whether she is being purchased out of slavery or redeemed out of prostitution.[5] The meaning is quite unclear. What is clear, however, is that the wife is purchased for a price, giving Hosea, the purchaser, the right to stipulate their relationship: "Thou shalt abide for me many days; thou shalt not play the harlot, and thou shalt not be for another man." This list of commands is followed by his statement of *his* responsibility: "So will I also be for thee" (Hosea 3:3). Notice the reciprocal nature of the covenant, both partners being bound to obligations of faithfulness. Violation of this covenant by either party would be adultery. Chapter 3, verse 4, prophesies Israel's long period of separation from the covenant, during which time of divorce the Israelites would enjoy neither direction from a king nor divine instruction through revelation. Finally, the children of Israel would return "and seek the Lord their God, . . . and shall fear the Lord and his goodness in the latter days" (Hosea 3:5).

The Controversy

Beginning in chapter 4 the marriage of Hosea is no longer a factor in his prophecy. But marriage remains the image through which his message is conveyed. Verse 1 is one of the most important verses in the book: "Hear the word of the Lord, ye children of Israel: for the Lord hath a controversy with the inhabitants of the land, because there is no truth, nor mercy, nor knowledge of God in the land." "Controversy" here is from the same root as the word inadequately translated "plead" in Hosea 2:2. "Plead" is not at all what Hosea had in mind. As has been explained elsewhere, "The verb *rîb* never describes an appeal or call to repentance, but always a hostile confrontation, an accusation. It refers to an angry quarrel or altercation, in any situation, with more formal application to disputation in a court of law. The verb can mean to lay charges, denounce, bring evidence, argue a case, viz. the actions of the aggrieved party."[6] In verse 1 the Lord does indeed accuse Israel. He brings legal proceedings against her for breach of covenant and takes her to divorce court. The specific charges brought against Israel are threefold: "There is no truth, nor mercy, nor knowledge of God in the land." We must examine these three concepts—truth, mercy, and knowledge—individually.

First of all, "truth." The Hebrew word from which it is translated, *'emet*, means more than just truth. It means also honesty, integrity, stability, and permanence. It is the kind of permanent honesty that stands at the core of any covenant or marriage relationship. This, according to Jehovah, is lacking on the part of his spouse.

Second, "mercy." The Hebrew word from which this is translated is *ḥesed*. "Mercy" is not a good translation; in fact, there is no English word that conveys the meaning of *ḥesed* accurately. It means loving-kindness or unfailing love. It is the kind of love that translates into action, a key requirement of a successful marriage.

Third, "knowledge." The Hebrew word *da'at* comes from the root *yd'* which means "to know." Yet this word means much more than "knowledge," both in a semantic and in a theological sense. Recall that the verb "to know" is used in the Bible to denote sexual relations. For example, "And Adam knew Eve his wife; and she conceived, and bare Cain" (Genesis 4:1). "And Adam knew his wife again; and she bare a son, and called his name Seth" (Genesis 4:25). Knowledge here denotes the most intimate possible relationship between two individuals, both physical and emotional. The sexual union is the most profound expression of oneness within the bond of marriage. It belongs exclusively within that bond and in the scriptures is strictly prohibited from any other context. Only in marriage is this ultimate intimacy appropriate. It is therefore most fitting that Hosea should allude to it in his teachings concerning the exclusive intimacy of the covenant bond between Jehovah and his chosen people.

Each of the three terms defined above is found in Hosea 2:19-20, which describes the reestablishment of the covenant, or the remarriage, following the divorce. "Lovingkindness" is translated from *ḥesed;* the same word is rendered "mercy" in Hosea 4:1. "Faithfulness" comes from the same root, and means essentially the same thing, as "truth" in Hosea 4:1. And the concept of "knowing" the Lord is found in both passages. These qualities are key aspects[7] of the religion of ancient Israel. When they are present, the covenant faith is intact. When they are gone, the covenant faith is lost.

Earlier in this study I mentioned three fundamental promises, implied or stated, that form the foundation of a successful marriage: honesty, unfailing love, and strict faithfulness. These are precisely the qualities mentioned in Hosea 4:1. God's controversy with Israel is based on the fact that they are missing from the relationship. And when those fundamentals are absent, the conditions described in the next verse come to the fore: swearing, lying, killing, stealing, and committing adultery. All five of these are prohibited in the Ten Commandments, which is "a list of things necessary to preserve the tranquil continuation of society."[8] As these evils become the norm, society rapidly becomes chaotic and disintegrates. Both the Old Testament and the Book of Mormon bear witness, through sad example, that this tragic cycle results when the covenant with God is broken.

The concept of "knowledge," used to describe the exclusive intimacy of the covenant bond, is very important. Hosea uses this concept in the sense of establishing and maintaining an intimate covenant relationship. Notice the following in Hosea 13:4-5 concerning the establishment of the covenant between Jehovah and Israel, expressed in the vocabulary of marriage. The translation is my own.

> I am Jehovah your god
> from the land of Egypt.

Egypt is where Jehovah found Israel, his bride.

> You shall *know* no god but me
> and there is no savior but me.

The use of the verb "know" here is important, as it refers to a relationship of great intimacy that Israel is permitted to have only with Jehovah in the bond of the covenant. Anything other than that is the equivalent of adultery.

> I *knew* you in the wilderness
> in the land of drought.

The wilderness refers to the Sinai desert, where God established the covenant with the Israelites. The marriage was performed there and the honeymoon took place there. In the imagery of Hosea, the exodus from Egypt and the covenants made in the Sinai wilderness represent Jehovah's finding his bride and marrying her by covenant. Their sojourn in the wilderness was the honeymoon. Notice that during the honeymoon, or the early stage of their union, the intimacy of God and Israel's *knowing* each other was a vibrant reality of their relationship: "I *knew* you in the wilderness" (vs. 5). But by Hosea's day, five hundred years later, things had changed. The honeymoon was over. Israel was sharing her intimacies promiscuously with other lovers. God rightly announced in Hosea 4:1 that he had a controversy with Israel because there was no "knowledge of God" in the land.

This is God's controversy with Israel. He is suing her for divorce on the grounds of adultery. Israel has not remained true to the covenants. Her infidelity has taken the form of worship of false gods and numerous other violations of God's commandments. As such, God is perfectly justified in terminating the covenant and canceling Israel's bride status. As he proclaimed through the Prophet Joseph Smith in a later age, "I, the Lord, am bound when ye do what I say; but when ye do not what I say, ye have no promise" (D&C 82:10). Yet through it all Jehovah has been strictly faithful to his covenant with Israel. He stated through Amos, "I *have known* only you of all the families of the earth" (Amos 3:2, my translation).

Apostasy as Adultery

A frequent characteristic of Hebrew prophecy is the description of apostasy through the metaphor of adultery. Adultery is, by definition, sexual relations with someone other than one's husband or wife. The national apostasy of Israel involved relations with (i.e., worship of) gods other than Jehovah. In the Old Testament, God is jealous of his relationship with his people and does not stand for Israel's sharing intimacies with others. Adultery, then, is the ideal metaphor for referring to that condition.

Several of the most powerful passages that concern the wickedness of Israel are couched in the imagery of adulterous behavior. The language in these passages is often explicit in describing the illicit sexual activities of Israel, personifying her not only as an adulteress but also as a "whore" or sometimes worse. In modern times we are not used to conceiving of God's speaking in the kinds of terms recorded by the ancient prophets. Our Western cultural heritage makes us uncomfortable when discussing certain things in public, particularly those relating to sexual matters. These inhibitions were not shared to the same degree by the peoples of the ancient Near East, and the Israelites, including God's prophets, were no exception. They freely spoke of the sins of Israel in ways that to our ears sound not only blunt but obscene. In most cases,

God is the speaker. I will examine only a few examples, not as an illustration of the culture of the ancient world, but to show how the Lord through his prophets chose to express his utter disgust for Israel's behavior in the strongest conceivable terms.

We have already seen how Hosea characterized Israel not only as an adulteress but as a prostitute, since she accepted bread, water, wool, flax, oil, drink (all in Hosea 2:5), vines, and trees (Hosea 2:12) in exchange for sexual favors to her lovers. Jeremiah accused Israel of having "gone up upon every high mountain and under every green tree," and there having "played the harlot" (Jeremiah 3:6). Her sister Judah was accused of committing adultery "with stones and with stocks" (Jeremiah 3:9).

The most graphic discussions of Israel's collective apostasy are found in Ezekiel, chapters 16 and 23. I use here the New International Version, since it conveys the Lord's words more clearly and more faithfully to the original Hebrew than does the King James text. We will consider chapter 16 first.

The allegory in Ezekiel 16 tells how Israel, the daughter of an Amorite and a Hittite, was left to die in an open field on the day of her birth. Jehovah found her, still covered with blood and with her umbilical cord not yet cut, saved her life, and caused her to grow up and become a beautiful woman. When she was mature, he established a covenant with her, depicted as the consummation of their marriage (see Ezekiel 16:8). He dressed her in beautiful clothing and adorned her in the finest of jewelry. Her fame spread among the nations because of the perfect beauty which God had given her. But soon Israel began misusing that beauty: "But you trusted in your beauty and used your fame to become a prostitute. You lavished your favors on anyone who passed by and your beauty became his." (Ezekiel 16:15.) In verse 22 the Lord laments, "In all your detestable practices and your prostitution you did not remember the days of your youth when you were naked and bare, kicking about in your blood." Then the divine complaint continues (Ezekiel 16:23-29):

> Woe! Woe to you, declares the Sovereign Lord.
> In addition to all your other wickedness, you built a mound for yourself and made a lofty shrine in every public square.
> At the head of every street you built your lofty shrines and degraded your beauty, offering your body with increasing promiscuity to anyone who passed by.

You engaged in prostitution with the Egyptians, your lustful neighbors, and provoked me to anger with your increasing promiscuity.

So I stretched out my hand against you and reduced your territory; I gave you over to the greed of your enemies, the daughters of the Philistines, who were shocked by your lewd conduct.

You engaged in prostitution with the Assyrians too, because you were insatiable; and even after that, you still were not satisfied.

Then you increased your promiscuity to include Babylonia, a land of merchants, but even with this you were not satisfied.

Israel is depicted as having an insatiable appetite for sexual gratification. She situated herself at the head of every street and offered her body to anyone who passed by. She was promiscuous with Egypt, Assyria, and Babylonia. But still she could not be satisfied. Even the Philistines, who in the Old Testament are almost the embodiment of wickedness, were shocked by her lewd conduct. Then the Lord's denunciation of his adulterous wife continues. He accuses her of being even worse than just a prostitute. Prostitutes at least receive payment for their favors. Israel does the opposite: she pays anyone who passes by to have sexual relations with her.[9]

Ezekiel chapter 23 paints a similar picture of the immoral character of the house of Israel, using a somewhat different allegory. Here the two kingdoms, Israel and Judah, are characterized as two sisters who were immoral before Jehovah found them in Egypt and who failed to change their ways after he married them. The elder sister, Israel, lusted after the Assyrians, whose splendor and virility she could not resist, and gave herself to them just as she had to the Egyptians when she was younger. In the Lord's words, "She gave herself as a prostitute to all the elite of the Assyrians and defiled herself with all the idols of everyone she lusted after. She did not give up the prostitution she began in Egypt, when during her youth men slept with her, caressed her virgin bosom and poured out their lust upon her." (Ezekiel 23:7-8.) But the younger sister, Judah, was even worse. Verse 11 says that "in her lust and prostitution she was more depraved than her sister." She also lusted after the Assyrians but went even further and lusted after the Babylonians as well. As the Lord states further:

> As soon as she saw them, she lusted after them and sent messengers to them in Chaldea.
>
> Then the Babylonians came to her, to the bed of love, and in their lust they defiled her. After she had been defiled by them, she turned away from them in disgust.
>
> When she carried on her prostitution openly and exposed her nakedness, *I* turned away from *her* in disgust, just as I had turned away from her sister.
>
> Yet she became more and more promiscuous as she recalled the days of her youth, when she was a prostitute in Egypt. (Ezekiel 23:16-19; italics added.)

There are still other examples in the Bible of apostasy described as whoredom or adultery,[10] but these will suffice. The Lord's use of this metaphor is not arbitrary or meaningless. It is ideal; it is the most profound way possible to characterize the behavior of Israel, who promiscuously violated the vows of the covenant by giving herself to the worship of other gods. From Jehovah's perspective this is adultery, the ultimate insult and sadness to him.

Punishment, Repentance, and Reunion

Adultery is a serious sin. The prophets' use of this metaphor to represent Israel's violation of her covenant with God shows that the gravity of her apostasy cannot be minimized. But adultery is not an unpardonable sin, nor is Israel's breach of covenant unpardonable. Yet Israel must be punished and must repent before Jehovah can take her back.

In Hosea 2 the punishment of the unfaithful wife is characterized by her allegorically being exposed and humiliated in front of her lovers, and also by the destruction of her false system of worship and the ruining of her land. In Ezekiel 16:37-41, the Lord pronounces the following sentence on her:

> Therefore I am going to gather all your lovers, with whom you found pleasure, those you loved as well as those you hated. I will gather them against you from all around and will strip you in front of them, and they will see all your nakedness.
>
> I will sentence you to the punishment of women who commit adultery and who shed blood; I will bring upon you the blood vengeance of my wrath and jealous anger.
>
> Then I will hand you over to your lovers, and they will tear down your mounds and destroy your lofty shrines. They will

strip you of your clothes and take your fine jewelry and leave you naked and bare.

They will bring a mob against you, who will stone you and hack you to pieces with their swords.

They will burn down your houses and inflict punishment on you in the sight of many women. I will put a stop to your prostitution, and you will no longer pay your lovers.

Even though this is allegorical for the most part, it is significant that the punishment was in fact brought upon both kingdoms, Israel and Judah, by those nations who were identified as their lovers, Assyria and Babylon. A more literal prophecy of the actual punishment that the Israelites would receive was given by Moses: "I call heaven and earth to witness against you this day, that ye shall soon utterly perish from off the land whereunto ye go over Jordan to possess it; ye shall not prolong your days upon it, but shall utterly be destroyed. And the Lord shall scatter you among the nations, and ye shall be left few in number among the heathen, whither the Lord shall lead you." (Deuteronomy 4:26-27.)

Destruction and scattering are Israel's punishment. She will remain scattered until she repents and comes back to Jehovah. Only when she enters anew into a covenant with him will her blessings of being a chosen people be restored (see 1 Nephi 19:15-16; 2 Nephi 6:11; 10:7-8). To some extent, the tribe of Joseph is being gathered again to Jehovah's covenant in The Church of Jesus Christ of Latter-day Saints. The gathering and restoration of Judah and the other tribes of Israel will not take place until they too repent and join the covenant with the Lord. God can raise up children to Abraham out of "stones" (Matthew 3:9), but he will not take his unfaithful wife back until she puts away her false worship and covenants to worship him alone.

Hosea's account of accepting his wife again after her repentance characterizes God's desire to take Israel back. Through Jeremiah he revealed the following words, a loving husband's compelling plea for the return of his wife who has badly wronged him:

Return, thou backsliding Israel, saith the Lord; and I will not cause mine anger to fall upon you: for I am merciful, saith the Lord, and I will not keep anger for ever.

Only acknowledge thine iniquity, that thou has transgressed against the Lord thy God, and hast scattered thy ways to the strangers under every green tree, and ye have not obeyed my voice, saith the Lord.

Turn, O backsliding children, saith the Lord; for I am married unto you. (Jeremiah 3:12-14.)

Notes

1. All biblical quotations are from the King James translation unless otherwise indicated.

2. For example, see H. H. Rowley, *Bulletin of the John Reylands Library* 39:200ff.; R. K. Harrison, *Introduction to the Old Testament* (Grand Rapids, Mich.: Eerdmans, 1969), pp. 861-68 and the references cited there.

3. Spencer W. Kimball, *The Miracle of Forgiveness* (Salt Lake City, Utah: Bookcraft, 1969).

4. Compare the discussion in Harrison, pp. 862-64, and F. I. Andersen and D. N. Freedman, *Hosea* (Garden City, N. Y.: Doubleday, 1980), pp. 298-300.

5. Andersen and Freedman, pp. 298-300.

6. Ibid., p. 219.

7. Or "representative elements"; ibid., p. 336.

8. G. E. Mendenhall in a personal communication to the author.

9. The King James Version term "whoredom" more accurately expresses Ezekiel's original intent than does "prostitution" of the New International Version. "Prostitute" is a professional designation, whereas the word "whore" also expresses the strong *moral* judgment implied in Ezekiel's use of the Hebrew *zônâ* (e.g., see Ezekiel 16:35).

10. For example, see Jeremiah 3:6-11; Hosea 5:3-4.

4

Ezekiel: Prophet of Judgment, Prophet of Promise

Gerald N. Lund

As I looked over the assignment to cover the entire book of Ezekiel in a fifty-minute lecture, it occurred to me that the job is somewhat analogous to trying to guide a tour of Disneyland in one hour. If I were a guide and had to do that for you, I'd really come down to one of two options. One way to do it would be to go inside the park and in that hour's time, running as fast as we could, try to see as many things as possible, by necessity choosing only the highlights—maybe Pirates of the Caribbean, or the Matterhorn, or the Haunted House. Then our time would be gone. We would just have to say, "When you come back be sure and see this or that." But there is another option for the guide who really desires to be helpful. At Disneyland there is a monorail which goes all the way around the outside of the park. A guide could spend the hour with you on the monorail, going around and orienting you to the design and layout of the park, pointing out what to look for and how to enjoy it when you get more time to go back.

The same problems are encountered in trying to cover Ezekiel in an hour's time. We can choose three or four special areas, focus on them in some detail, and tell you that the rest are also interesting. Or we can give an overview, orienting you to the layout of the book, so that when you return to it with more time you can find your own way about.

Obviously, if that is really what we are limited to, both options have their frustrations and their drawbacks. But I choose the second option. We are going to discuss the book of Ezekiel using the "monorail" approach. I accept the inherent frustrations in that approach with the hope that, when you come back to Ezekiel on your own, you will be better oriented, will know what to look for, and will therefore have a more meaningful experience.

As I look at the book of Ezekiel, I find four points of orientation that help us chart our course. They are all interdependent and interwoven, but still can be seen as four ways to view Ezekiel. They are: (1) Ezekiel the man, (2) Ezekiel the captive, (3) Ezekiel the answerer, and (4) Ezekiel the writer.

Ezekiel the Man

Considering the length of his book, we know surprisingly little about Ezekiel the man. His name means "God strengthens,"[1] or, as one scholar translated it, "God will prevail" or "whom God has strengthened."[2] This name is significant and appropriate.

We know from his own record that he was the son of Buzi (unfortunately we don't know who Buzi was), and that he was a priest (Ezekiel 1:3). Almost certainly he was carried away captive into Babylon in the second group of captives taken by Nebuchadnezzar (see 2 Kings 24:10-16). Some scholars have speculated that he may have served in the temple in Jerusalem before he was taken captive into Babylon, because in the later chapters it is obvious that he is intimately familiar with the temple rituals and other things that took place there. But he himself makes no mention of it, so that is merely speculation.

Josephus says that Ezekiel was carried away when he was young, implying that he may have been a young man or even a boy.[3] That he was a boy doesn't seem likely, however, for several reasons. First, it was in the fifth year of his exile that he was called to be a prophet (Ezekiel 1:2). Second, in chapter 4, verse 14, Ezekiel spoke of his youth as though it was long past. Third, in the ninth year of his captivity, Ezekiel's wife died (Ezekiel 24:16-18), which again would seem to imply that he was a little older man. Finally, Ezekiel 1:1 contains an interesting phrase to consider: "Now it came to pass in the *thirtieth* year, in the fourth month, in the fifth day of the month'' (emphasis added). Though Ezekiel doesn't say the thirtieth year of what, some scholars have assumed that maybe it was the thirtieth year of his own life. If that were the case, he would have been about twenty-five when he was taken into captivity. However, if it refers to the thirtieth year of his captivity, we cannot say for sure how old he was. (See similar dating references in Ezekiel 29:17; 31:1; etc.)

In two or three places in Ezekiel, we learn that while he was in exile the elders of the Jews came to his home to counsel with him (for example, see Ezekiel 8:1; 14:1; 20:1). Most often they rejected his counsel, but it is interesting that he functioned as a prophet in a very personal, face-to-face setting. It was for this reason that one scholar referred to him as a ''pastor as well as prophet.''[4]

We know from Ezekiel's own record that he lived among the exiles in Tel Abib (Ezekiel 1:1, 3; 3:15), which seems to have been a colony of the Jewish exiles on the river Chebar, probably a small tributary of the Euphrates a little east of the city of Babylon itself. He spent his life among the captives, and the record indicates that he ministered for at least twenty-two years after his call as a prophet. Some questionable traditions indicate that he died a martyr at the hands of one of the Jewish leaders offended by his prophecies.[5] Beyond that we know virtually nothing more about Ezekiel the man.

However, the Book of Mormon provides one additional interesting insight. In 1 Nephi 1:4, Nephi writes, ''For it came to pass in the commencement of the first year of the reign of Zedekiah, king of Judah, (my father Lehi, having dwelt at Jerusalem in all his days); and *in that same year there came many prophets,* prophesying unto the people that they must repent, or the great city Jerusalem must be destroyed'' (emphasis added). Ezekiel was contemporary with Lehi and could easily have been one of those prophets. We know the names of four of the prophets of that day— Lehi, Ezekiel, Jeremiah, and Daniel. Lehi's call was to lead a colony out of Jerusalem to a promised land. Jeremiah's call was to stay and bear witness of the destruction of Jerusalem. Daniel was called into exile, but he went into the royal courts and there was allowed to get a picture of the grand world view of history. Ezekiel was called to go among the captives and explain to them why this terrible tragedy had happened.

Ezekiel the Captive

When I talk about Ezekiel the captive, I refer to the historical setting in which he lived and wrote. And to do that I first need to talk about some historical and prophetic antecedents which are relevant to his time. Then we also need to explain the historical setting in which Ezekiel was found.

Probably the most important historical and prophetic antecedent dates back to Moses and his warnings to the people of Israel as they entered the promised land. Leviticus 26 and Deuteronomy 28 are whole chapters warning the people that once they entered the land of promise they would incur a solemn obligation. As long as they were faithful, righteous, and committed to the covenant, Moses promised them blessings. The land would be blessed, their enemies would be set aside, and so on (see Leviticus 26:1-13; Deuteronomy 28:1-14). But if they broke that covenant, then Moses began a series of grim warnings (see Leviticus 26:14-39; Deuteronomy 28:15-68). In both chapters Moses warned that the conditions would be such that cannibalism would result (see Leviticus 26:29; Deuteronomy 28:53, 57). That prophecy was fulfilled not once but several times (see 2 Kings 6:29; Lamentations 4:9-10).[6]

The second historical precedent was the echoing of Moses' warning by virtually every prophet after Moses. Joshua, Elijah, Elisha, Isaiah, Amos, Hosea, Micah—everywhere we look, the prophets are found reminding Israel of the basic choice: either be faithful and reap blessings or be unfaithful and reap curses and punishments. The third historical prophetic antecedent occurred approximately one hundred years before Ezekiel's time when the Northern Kingdom was taken captive by Assyria. It was destroyed, annihilated—it ceased to exist. The people were taken north into Assyria, scattered and assimilated, and lost to history. At the time when the Northern Kingdom fell, the southern border of the kingdom of Assyria was five miles north of Jerusalem. Judah escaped the fate of the Northern Kingdom only by divine intervention because King Hezekiah heeded the counsel of the prophet Isaiah. (See 2 Kings 18-19; Isaiah 36-37.) Sennacherib laid siege to Jerusalem. Isaiah told Hezekiah not to worry, that not a single arrow would be fired against the city. And that night, in the quaint translation of the King James Version, 185,000 people woke up dead (see 2 Kings 19:35) and so Judah was delivered.

That event should have been such a graphic demonstration of the principle of spiritual survival—turn to God and live or face destruction—that Judah would have repented. But less than a century later, we find Judah back in the same state of wickedness facing a similar threat of destruction at the hands of Babylon. That is what we mean by the historical/prophetic antecedents of Ezekiel's time. He knew the warnings, he knew the doctrine, he knew the inevitable certainties if Judah did not repent.

Now let us look at the historical setting of Ezekiel's own day. In 612 B.C., Babylon began to seriously challenge the might of Assyria. Assyria was in a state of serious decay, so Babylonia moved north, and in 612 B.C. Nineveh fell. Basically that signaled the end of the Assyrian Empire. In 609 B.C. Egypt, preferring a weak Assyria to a strong Babylonia, made an alliance with Assyria. When the final battle between those two empires began, Egypt moved north to side with Assyria. It was at that time, though the scriptural record doesn't say why, that the righteous King Josiah of Judah tried to stop Pharaoh Necho at Megiddo. As nearly as we can tell it was like a fly trying to stop a bull. Necho swatted the fly and moved on, leaving Josiah dead and Judah mourning (see 2 Kings 23:29-30; 2 Chronicles 35:20-24). Though Assyria was destroyed, the battle between Egypt and Babylon ended more or less in a draw. Pharaoh Necho made Judah a vassal state, appointed King Jehoiakim as his puppet king, and made Judah pay tribute (see 2 Kings 23:31-35).

But Babylon was not through with Egypt. In 605 B.C., in what is called one of the significant battles of history, Egypt challenged Babylon in the battle of Carchemish. This time Babylon crushed Egypt and drove her all the way down into the plains of Philistia, which bordered Judah on the west. While he was there King Nebuchadnezzar, having decided that he would teach this state of Judah who their new master was, besieged Jerusalem. Jerusalem was no match for his power and therefore capitulated easily. Nebuchadnezzar withdrew, taking a small group of captives back with him to Babylon. This was the first of three times captives were taken. Daniel was almost certainly taken to Babylon in this first group.

Even though Jehoiakim was now a vassal king to Babylon, for some reason not fully explained in the scriptures he still gave his allegiance to Egypt. Both Jeremiah and Ezekiel warned that Egypt was weak and not to be trusted (see Jeremiah 44:29-30; 46:1-2; Ezekiel 17:15; 29:3, 19). Surprisingly, Egypt and Babylon clashed again in 601 B.C., but fought to a standstill this time. So Nebuchadnezzar withdrew back to Babylon. Ignoring the prophetic warnings, Jehoiakim decided that Babylon wasn't nearly as strong as Nebuchadnezzar had claimed, and he openly switched his allegiance to Egypt and stopped paying tribute to Babylon.

About 598 B.C. (traditional dating) Nebuchadnezzar decided to teach Judah a lesson. He laid siege to Jerusalem, killed King Jehoiakim, threw his body off the walls,[7] and took three thousand captives. Jehoiachin was appointed as the successor king.

In 2 Kings 24 we read the final outcome of this event. The passage beginning in verse 14 is particularly noteworthy in our study of Ezekiel: "And he carried away all Jerusalem, and all the princes, and all the mighty men of valour, even ten thousand captives, and all the craftsmen and smiths: none remained, save the poorest sort of the people of the land.

"And he carried away Jehoiachin to Babylon, and the king's mother, and the king's wives, and his officers, and the mighty of the land, those carried he into captivity from Jerusalem to Babylon.

"And all the men of might, even seven thousand, and craftsmen and smiths a thousand," and so on, and so on.

So Nebuchadnezzar virtually took the entire upper and middle classes of Jerusalem captive. Ezekiel, being a priest, was certainly included. Even though Ezekiel was now in Babylon, the events in Jerusalem still affected him and his work and are therefore of interest to us.

During the next ten years, Zedekiah, who was appointed to replace Jehoiachin as the ruler in Jerusalem, did not learn a thing from the previous tragedy, nor did Judah. In Jerusalem, false prophets began to abound, predicting that Babylon would be overthrown and the captives returned. While both Jeremiah and Ezekiel strongly denounced these men (see Jeremiah 28, 29; Ezekiel 13), their presence added to the general confusion abounding in Jerusalem.

Then a second interesting event happened. Two prophets, Jeremiah and Ezekiel, reportedly uttered "contradictory" prophecies. Because these two prophecies seemed to directly contradict each other, Zedekiah rationalized that the two true prophets couldn't be trusted and went on listening to the false prophets. Let's examine the "contradictory" prophecies.

Jeremiah 34:2-3 says: "Thus saith the Lord, the God of Israel; Go and speak to Zedekiah king of Judah, and tell him, Thus saith the Lord; Behold, I will give this city into the hand of the king of Babylon, and he shall burn it with fire:

"And thou [Zedekiah] shalt not escape out of his hand, but shalt surely be taken, and delivered into his hand; [and then notice this phrase] *and thine eyes shall behold the eyes of the king of Babylon,* and he shall speak with thee mouth to mouth, and thou shalt go to Babylon" (emphasis added). That is Jeremiah's prophecy.

But in Ezekiel 12:13, Ezekiel said of Zedekiah, "My net also will I spread upon him, and he shall be taken in my snare: and I will bring him to Babylon to the land of the Chaldeans; *yet shall he not see it,* though he shall die there" (emphasis added).

It is obvious why the king thought the two prophets contradicted each other. Jeremiah said Zedekiah would look into the eyes of the king of Babylon, while Ezekiel said he would be taken into the land of the Chaldeans but would not see it, even though he would die there.

But of course they did not contradict each other. The fulfillment is an interesting one. When Nebuchadnezzar came a third time and conquered Jerusalem in 587 B.C., his generals captured all of the nobles, including Zedekiah and his sons (except Mulek, who escaped), and brought them north to the encampment of their king. Nebuchadnezzar came face to face with his prisoners (so they looked into his eyes) and killed the sons of Zedekiah as Zedekiah watched. Then he put out Zedekiah's eyes, blinding him, and carried him away captive into Babylon. Thus both predictions were fulfilled: Zedekiah looked into the eyes of the Babylonian king, yet he never saw the land of Babylon, where he was carried captive and later died.

But whatever the cause, Zedekiah and Judah did not repent. Again they revolted against Babylon, and so in 589 B.C. Nebuchadnezzar returned. This time he said, in effect, "We'll provide a lesson that everyone will listen to. Let us show the world what happens to those who rebel against Babylon." He left Jerusalem leveled and in ruins, and Judah was no more.

That is the historical setting in which Ezekiel lived and prophesied. Without an understanding of those circumstances, the meaning of Ezekiel's writings will largely remain obscure.[8]

Ezekiel the Answerer

In the face of Nebuchadnezzar's successes in Palestine and the eventual fall of Judah, four important questions naturally arose in the minds of the people.

1. *Is Jerusalem really going to be destroyed?* In those last ten years of the reign of Zedekiah, that question was asked again and again. This was partly because the false prophets were confusing the people and partly because the Jews couldn't believe "God's people" would ever fall.

2. *If God is really God, and we are really his chosen people, why is he allowing this to happen?*

3. *If we are being destroyed for being like the other nations* (which Ezekiel and other prophets had said many times), *then why aren't those nations destroyed?*

4. *What will this tragedy mean for the covenant?* What will happen to all of the promises God has made about Israel's eventual triumph and salvation?

Now, those are some profound questions, and Ezekiel answered each one of them. And in fact, it is in understanding those questions and seeing how Ezekiel sought to answer them that we gain the greatest insights into his book. As much of his work is aimed at answering those questions, let's take them one at a time.

1. *Is Jerusalem really going to be destroyed?* Ezekiel gives an unqualified, resounding, thundering, yes! It is the major theme of chapters 4, 5, 6, 7, 8, 9, 11, 12, 15, 19, 21, 22, and 24. They all say Jerusalem has had it. That is a pretty hard answer to miss. Ezekiel himself went through several typological or symbolic actions to dramatize the coming disaster. For example, in chapter 4 he took a tile and drew a picture of Jerusalem on it. Then he put an iron pan against it. In that same chapter, by command of the Lord, he had to lie on his side for so many days, symbolizing the captivity, and

then he was told to cook his bread with cow dung to symbolize that the people in Judah would eat defiled bread in coming times. In chapter 5 Ezekiel cut his hair and divided it into thirds, burning some and scattering some, again symbolizing what the people would suffer. In chapter 12 he moved his whole household, showing that the house of Judah was going to be moved out of their dwelling place in Jerusalem.

In chapter 24 we read that Ezekiel's wife died on the very day Nebuchadnezzar besieged Jerusalem (see vss. 1-2). Here was given the ultimate symbol or type of Jerusalem's coming destruction. Beginning in verse 15, note what the Lord told him: "Also the word of the Lord came unto me, saying,

"Son of man, behold, I take away from thee the desire of thine eyes [that is a Hebrew euphemism for wife] with a stroke: *yet neither shalt thou mourn nor weep, neither shall thy tears run down.*

"Forbear to cry, make no mourning for the dead, bind the tire of thine head upon thee, and put on thy shoes upon thy feet, and cover not thy lips, and eat not the bread of men.

"So I spake unto the people in the morning: and at even my wife died; and I did in the morning [within twelve hours of his wife's death!] as I was commanded." (Emphasis added.)

Isn't that something? The Lord said in essence that the death of Ezekiel's wife would serve as a type and symbol of Jerusalem's destruction. When the people saw his wife die and saw that Ezekiel did not mourn, they asked why. In verse 22 the answer was given: "Ye shall do as I have done: ye shall not cover your lips, nor eat the bread of men." And then in verse 24 the Lord explained: "Thus Ezekiel is unto you a sign: according to all that he hath done shall ye do." Jerusalem was the bride of Jehovah, but there could be no mourning, for her tragedy was just and fully deserved.

So in answer to the people's first question, "Will Jerusalem really be destroyed?" Ezekiel gives a clear and unmistakable answer—yes.

2. *If God is really God, and we are really his chosen people, why is he allowing this to happen?* To this second question, once again Ezekiel answers that God *is* God and Israel *is* the covenant people. But they have rejected the covenant through wickedness;

therefore, the Lord allows these things to happen. Note how clearly Ezekiel responds to this second question:

Ezekiel 5:8: It is the Lord specifically who executes these judgments.

Ezekiel 7:4: The Lord not only refuses to have pity but specifically states, "I will recompense thy ways upon thee."

Ezekiel 7:19: Riches and wealth were "the stumblingblock of their iniquity."

Ezekiel 8: This entire chapter is devoted to a vision of the wickedness of Judah, including rampant idolatry which had even found its way into the temple (see esp. vss. 3-10). The Lord concludes by saying, "*Therefore* [because of this wickedness] will I also deal in fury" (vs. 18).

Ezekiel 16: This chapter contains a scathing denunciation of Israel. The chosen people are described as an illegitimate child; the Lord not only took her in (vss. 3-9) but adorned her like a bride (vss. 10-14) and married her himself. Instead of being faithful to her marriage to Jehovah, Israel played the part of the harlot (vs. 15), whoring after false gods. Indeed, the Lord said, she was worse than a harlot, for such a woman is unfaithful because her lovers give her money and gifts. In her spiritual adultery, Israel actually gave gifts to her lovers—the false gods (vss. 26-34). Then in that same chapter, in equally vivid imagery (see vss. 44-59), the Lord compared Judah to her spiritual sisters, Samaria (i.e., the northern kingdom of Israel, now lost and destroyed) and Sodom (the epitome of spiritual corruption).

And so Ezekiel's answer to the second question thunders out again and again. Judah and Jerusalem will reap the whirlwind they have sown in wickedness for generations. In chapter 33, Ezekiel gives one of the most profound and clear expositions of why judgments come upon a people. Clearly, Ezekiel explains, God takes no pleasure in sending these judgments, but the people leave him no choice. Note especially the language of verses 10-11.

3. The third question raised by the tragedy of Judah has to do with the surrounding nations. The Lord often noted that the Jews were no different than their neighbors. Because they had committed whoredoms with Egypt, Assyria, and the Chaldeans, they were facing destruction. That is understandable, but the spinoff question is, *why doesn't God destroy the other nations too?*

Ezekiel answers this question in two ways. The first answer is based on the principle taught in Doctrine and Covenants 82:3, that "unto whom much is given much is required; and he who sins against the greater light receives the greater condemnation." Note how Ezekiel repeatedly reminded the people that they were the Lord's chosen, that they had the law and the covenant. They were not like the Gentiles in light and knowledge, but they had lowered themselves to maintain the same standards of behavior. (The following references are only a brief sampling of many where Ezekiel teaches this principle: Ezekiel 3:4-7; 5:5-7; 8:17-18; 9:9; 13:2-10; 16:6-9, 15; 20:5.) So his first answer to the third question is simply: You have greater light than they; therefore, more is required of you.

His second answer is also clear and simple: Whoever said that the other nations are exempt from the wrath of the Lord? Chapters 25 to 32 and chapter 35 describe the judgments that would come or had already come upon Ammon, Moab, Edom, Philistia, Tyre, Sidon, Egypt, Assyria, and Babylon. While these nations were sometimes used by the Lord as the rods for punishing Israel, Ezekiel's prophecies show that they were not exempt from his judgments either.

4. The fourth question which arises out of the tragedy of these times asks: *If Jerusalem is destroyed, if the temple is lost, if we are scattered among the Gentiles, what does this mean for the covenant? Are we totally rejected by God? Are the promises and prophecies now set aside?*

In his answer to the first three questions Ezekiel is a "prophet of judgment," but his answers to this final question make him a "prophet of promise." A careful study of his writings shows that even the most harsh and caustic predictions and judgments were counterbalanced by an immediate addendum of hope. For example, after making dire and specific predictions of Jerusalem's destruction through famine, pestilence, war, and cannibalism (see Ezekiel 5:5-17), after predicting that Israel will be smitten with such devastation that the bones of the people will lie unburied before the altars of their false gods (see Ezekiel 6:4-5), the Lord tells Ezekiel: "*Yet* will I leave a remnant. . . . And they that escape of you shall remember me among the nations. . . . And they shall know that I am the Lord." (Ezekiel 6:8-10.)

ers 7 through 11 give an unremitting, uncompromising
Judah's wickedness and the consequent fury of the Lord
—desolation, war, pestilence, destruction, widespread slaughter,
and the carrying away of the survivors into captivity. But then
again, once the Lord has poured out a picture of grim and stark
despair he immediately, with two simple words, changes the tone.
"*Although* I have cast them far off . . . *yet* will I be to them as a
. . . sanctuary" (Ezekiel 11:16). Then follows a specific prophecy
of Israel's restoration—a prophecy of great hope and tremendous
promise:

> Therefore say, Thus saith the Lord God; I will even gather
> you from the people, and assemble you out of the countries
> where ye have been scattered, and I will give you the land of
> Israel.
> And they shall come thither, and they shall take away all the
> detestable things thereof and all the abominations thereof from
> thence.
> And I will give them one heart, and I will put a new spirit
> within you; and I will take the stony heart out of their flesh, and
> will give them an heart of flesh:
> That they may walk in my statutes, and keep mine ordi-
> nances, and do them: and they shall be my people, and I will be
> their God. (Ezekiel 11:17-20.)

This pattern of judgment and hope is repeated over and over.
Earlier in this article, mention was made of the scathing denunciation of Judah in chapter 16, where the covenant people are compared to a harlot and to the cities of Sodom and Samaria. The
words almost smoke even after twenty-six centuries. And yet when
the denunciation was finished, there followed a promise of the
restoration of the everlasting covenant, beginning with the hope-
laden word "nevertheless" (Ezekiel 16:60-63).

Additionally, we find in Ezekiel's writings some of the grandest
and most promising prophecies of Israel's future restoration and
acceptance by the Lord:

1. Israel will return to the covenant and experience an eventual
conversion to the gospel (Ezekiel 6:8-10; 11:17-20; 16:60-63;
17:22-24; 20:33-44; 33:11-16; 36:25-28; 37:1-14).

2. Israel will again have true prophets, loving pastors, and even
the Messiah, the new David, to rule over them and teach them
(Ezekiel 34:16-25; 37:24-28).

3. The land of Israel will be blessed and become fruitful, productive, and *inhabited* again (Ezekiel 33:26-28; 36:33-35; 47:1-11).

4. Latter-day scripture will be joined with the writings of Judah (Ezekiel 37:15-20).

5. Joseph and Judah will become one nation again, united under the gospel covenant (Ezekiel 37:21-25).

6. The temple will be rebuilt in Jerusalem again (Ezekiel 37:26-28; chapters 40-47).

7. The nations of the world will gather against Israel, but will be defeated through the help of the Lord, bringing in an era of peace and triumph for them (Ezekiel 38-39).

8. Israel will receive the land of promise as their permanent inheritance (Ezekiel 47-48).

What a message of hope and inspiration, and note how directly each of those prophecies serves to answer these questions. Has the Lord forgotten Israel? Is the covenant no longer valid? Are the chosen people to be destroyed? Is the promised land lost forever? Thus we can truly call Ezekiel the prophet of judgment *and* promise.

Ezekiel the Writer

Our final area of examination is to look at the organization of Ezekiel's book. The text gives no clue to who collected and organized his writings into the book we now find in the Old Testament. It may have been Ezekiel himself, but whoever did it seems to have understood the four basic questions and Ezekiel's answers to them. Note the following structure:

Chapters 1-3	God is God, he is real and has all power. He has called me, Ezekiel, as his prophet.
Chapters 4-24	Because of idolatry, wickedness, and rejection of the covenant, Jerusalem is going to be destroyed and Israel scattered.
Chapters 25-32	The surrounding nations are likewise going to reap the judgments of God because of their wickedness.
Chapters 33-48	But God will still fulfill the covenants he made with the ancient patriarchs. Israel will not be totally destroyed. In the future they will be restored to their lands, con-

verted to the true covenant, have righteous
prophets, rebuild their temple, and accept
the Messiah as their ruler.

Summary and Conclusion

There you have it—a quick "monorail ride" around Ezekiel. I
admit that we have had to ignore much that is of great interest,
much that is of great worth. And while this approach has been
somewhat frustrating and incomplete, at least I hope you will
return at your own leisure to read the book of Ezekiel and to study
him in depth, using this introduction to help you find greater satis-
faction and fruitfulness.

Notes

1. J. D. Douglas, ed., *The New Bible Dictionary* (Grand Rapids, Mich.: Wm.
B. Eerdmans Publishing Co., 1962), p. 406.

2. Samuel Fallows, *The Popular and Critical Bible Encyclopedia,* 3 vols.
(Chicago: Howard-Severance Co., 1911), 1:639.

3. Flavius Josephus, *Josephus: Complete Works,* trans. William Whiston
(Grand Rapids, Mich.: Kregel Publications, 1960), *Antiquities of the Jews* 10.6.3.

4. James Hastings, ed., *Dictionary of the Bible* (New York: Charles Scrib-
ner's Sons, 1909), p. 251.

5. Ibid.; Fallows, 1:639.

6. See also Josephus, *Wars of the Jews,* 6.4.4.

7. Josephus, *Antiquities of the Jews,* 10.6.3.

8. For excellent summaries of this period of history see Harry Thomas Frank,
Discovering the Biblical World (New York: Harper and Row, 1975), pp. 124-30;
Michael Avi-Yonah, ed., *A History of the Holy Land* (Jerusalem: Jerusalem Pub-
lishing House, 1969), pp. 90-97; *Great People of the Bible and How They Lived*
(Pleasantville, N.Y.: Reader's Digest, 1974), pp. 230-45.

5

Jonah: Testimony of the Resurrection

LeGrande Davies

In Luke 11:29-32, Jesus says concerning the sign of Jonah:

> And when the people were gathered thick together, he began to say, This is an evil generation: they seek a sign; and there shall no sign be given it, but the sign of Jonah the prophet. For as Jonah was a sign unto the Ninevites, so also shall the Son of man be to this generation. The queen of the south shall rise up in the judgment with the men of this generation, and condemn them: for she came from the utmost parts of the earth to hear the wisdom of Solomon; and, behold, a greater than Solomon is here. The men of Nineveh shall rise up in the judgment with this generation, and shall condemn it: for they repented at the preaching of Jonah; and behold, a greater than Jonah is here.[1]

A similar statement is found in Matthew 12:39-41, except the Lord adds in verse 40, "For as Jonah was three days and three nights in the whale's belly; so shall the Son of man be three days and three nights in the heart of the earth." The King James Version says "whale," but the Greek word is *ketos,* which means "huge fish."[2]

Jesus declared that the sign of Jonah would witness his three days of death and burial in the grave and then his return to the world of the living. Matthew 16:4 contains another statement concerning the sign of Jonah. "A wicked and adulterous generation seeketh after a sign; and there shall no sign be given unto it, but the sign of the prophet Jonah. And he left them and departed." In

2 Kings 14:25 "Jonah the son of Amittai, the prophet" is mentioned as having prophesied concerning Jeroboam II. No other mention of Jonah is made in scripture, except in the small book of Jonah, which has always caused considerable stir in both academic and religious circles.

The book of Jonah, with four short chapters, is tremendously provocative in content. Stands concerning its authenticity and purpose have been debated extensively. Robert H. Pfeiffer declared, "The story of Jonah, written about 350 to 320 B.C., is not an account of actual happenings nor an allegory of the destiny of Israel nor of the Messiah. It is fiction, a short story with a moral."[3] Edward Young retorted:

> It should be noted that Christ believed in the historicity of the miracles recorded in Jonah and the historicity of the prophet's mission to the Ninevites. Hence we cannot regard the book as legendary and unhistorical in character. For the believer in Jesus, it is sufficient that in God's miraculous power the prophet was kept alive in the belly of a fish for three days.[4]

These two statements identify the two widely divergent extremes, both of which are equally inaccurate.

The critical reviews of the book of Jonah show as many conclusions as there are authors who have written about it. It has been concluded that the story of Jonah was nothing but a legend told by a good storyteller, or perhaps a "legendary narrative attached to a historical prophet in the reign of Jeroboam II by a later writer," and also that "the book was not nearly so old as the prophet and shows definite influences of Deutero-Isaiah."[5] It is "in no sense literal history," while for others it is in every sense literal. It is an allegory of the coming rebirth of the land of Israel, or of the Messiah; or it is merely a moralistic story or a typical hero cycle which Joseph Campbell calls the "Monomyth."

Each of these divergent conclusions has been reached by a different method of analysis: technical higher criticism, comparison with historical records, the presence or absence of archaeological evidences, but, most common, mere pronouncement. Regardless of the conclusions drawn or the methods used, only one general consensus prevails: There is no definite physical evidence known at the present time that can either prove or disprove the book of Jonah. Whether it is valid or invalid, historical or unhistorical, literal or allegorical, is strictly a matter of personal preference. It was with these divergent conclusions in mind that I decided to write this paper.

Latter-day Saints hold the basic premise that the book of Jonah is acceptable scripture and as such is "true." However, the questions "Did Jonah really live?" and "How was he able to survive in the belly of a whale?" are generally considered the most important issues related to the book of Jonah. "Fantastic stories" have been found, manipulated, and propounded to show the historicity of the book, and parallels of sailors surviving in whales' bellies are run past in endless display.[6] Few discussions are concerned with the context and commentary of the Savior when he made reference to Jonah in his preaching.

The basic story of Jonah is that of a prophet called by God to minister but who does not want to fulfill that calling. At the beginning of chapter 1 we find Jonah setting sail from the port of Joppa for Tarshish, which has been identified as Sardinia,[7] paying his own fare on a ship. Promptly after boarding the ship, he goes down into the hold and falls into a deep sleep. He is in this stupor of sleep until "the steersman" or "the master of the ship" awakens him and makes him arise, saying to him, "What are you sleeping for? Get up. Call upon your God. Don't you know that we are all about to perish?" (Jonah 1:7.) Jonah goes up onto the deck and finds the sailors about to cast lots to find out who—not what, but who—is the cause of the terrible storm that is upon them. The lot falls upon Jonah. They ask him, "Who are you? Where are you from? What God do you worship?" Their considerable curiosity seems centered in his relationship with his God and why his God would take such an interest in such a seemingly insignificant and common man. Why would the God of Israel be so angry with Jonah? What has he done that would make his God seek him out even outside the confines of his own country? And finally, they wondered what kind of a God had such power over the whole world. Jonah acknowledges that he is the cause of their problems, that he is a Hebrew and is trying to flee an appointment by the God of Israel. The last acknowledgment is rather moot, however, because, as is noted in Jonah 1:10, the crew already knew that he was trying to escape from his God when they took him on board. Admitting he is the cause of the storm, he asks them to throw him

overboard, but they refuse; instead they try to save him by
"rowing hard toward shore" (Jonah 1:13). Unsuccessful, they
pray to the Lord in essence:

> Lord, we recognize that you must be the God of all the world,
> we understand Jonah has a problem with you. We don't want
> you to hold us accountable for this man's death or his problem.
> We are going to throw him overboard. He is in your hands to do
> as you see fit.

They do, and Jonah is swallowed by a great fish (the word *dag
gadol* is used here, meaning a large or great fish). For three days
and three nights he is in the belly of that large fish. "Then Jonah
prayed unto the Lord his God out of the fish's belly" (Jonah 2:1),
but his prayer or psalm is uttered in such a way as to show that by
this time he is already out of the fish. He says:

> I called to the Lord in my distress,
> and he answered me;
> out of the belly of Sheol I cried for help,
> and thou hast heard my cry.
>
> (Jonah 2:2.)

The term *Sheol,* or hell, is used here as a direct reference to what
Latter-day Saints call the spirit world. *Sheol* should not be defined
as most Christian denominations define hell; it is strictly the place
where the spirits of all people go when they die. J. H. Hertz indicates that "*Sheol* [is] the name of the abode of the dead."[8] Thus,
the conclusion elucidated by the Hebrew text, Jonah was dead! In
that condition his spirit continued to pray, being fearful about the
things that were happening and would continue to happen to him.
He cried that the water was closing around his neck and he was
sinking into a world whose bars would hold him fast forever. He
was sinking fast into an eternal damnation; an eternal as well as a
physical death. He was afraid that he would be permanently dead,
that the gift of escape promised in Psalms would not be available to
him.

> Therefore my heart exults
> and my spirit exults and my spirit rejoices,
> my body too rests unafraid;
> for thou wilt not abandon me in *Sheol*
> nor suffer thy faithful servant to see the pit.
>
> (Psalm 30:4; see also 86:13; 16:10.)

Then Jonah, stretched to his final breaking point, declared his allegiance to the Lord and his recognition that his salvation had come from the Lord.

> I was sinking into the world
> whose bars would hold me fast forever.
> But thou didst bring me up alive from the pit, O Lord my God.
>   As my senses failed me I remembered the Lord,
> and my prayer reached thee in thy holy temple.
>   Men who worship false gods may abandon their loyalty,
>   But I will offer thee sacrifice with words of praise.
> I will pay my vows; victory is the Lord's.
>   Then the Lord spoke to the fish
> and it spewed Jonah out onto dry land.
>   (Jonah 2:6-10.)

Jonah's saga continues as he goes to the city of Nineveh. As a "prophet" he calls the people to repentance. When they repent, Jonah, strangely enough, is not pleased, but would rather that God destroy them. He then prays to the Lord, demanding Nineveh's destruction. The image comes to mind of Jonah sitting on top of the hill rubbing his hands together and saying, "Get them, Lord. You know I preached to them, now get them." When God refuses, Jonah becomes very angry, saying:

> I knew that thou art "a god gracious and compassionate, long-suffering and ever constant, and willing to turn away the disaster" [here he is quoting Exodus 34:6].
>   And now, Lord, take my life: I should be better dead than alive. (Jonah 4:2-3.)

This last statement sounds almost like the cry of Elijah when he felt he had failed in his mission (see 1 Kings 19). Jonah's perception of his mission was different from the Lord's and he tried to force his ideas on the Lord. He wanted to destroy the people of Nineveh, but God forgave them. In the midst of Jonah's rebellion, the Lord introduces a *kikion* tree, to grow up, shelter and protect Jonah from the heat of the sun,[9] for which Jonah is very grateful. But in the night a worm eats out the inside of the plant, and when the sun comes up and the hot east winds or "death winds" off the deserts blow, it withers and dies. To Jonah's distress God then asks, "Are you so angry over the *kikion?*" "Yes," Jonah answers, "I am very angry about it." The Lord replies, "You are sorry for

ou didn't have any part in growing it. It is a plant
the night and withered in the night, and why should
or feel concerned for the great city of Nineveh?''
1.)

ned story of Jonah seems like a nice little ''myth,''
''herc ̣ ʒ,'' or ''miracle story'' that doesn't seem to merit all the
concern given it.

Meaning and interpretations of scripture have always been considered on at least two parallel levels: the literal and the spiritual.
Umberto Cassuto has stated that this ''parallelism is apparently
intended by scripture in accordance with its principle that the
experiences of the fathers foreshadow those of the descendents.''[10]
This should be considered the rudiment principle for understanding the structure of all scriptures. Thus Jonah's importance is
governed as much by his power for foreshadowing the lives of the
''descendents'' as it is by his literal being.

Typological interpretation was recognized by ancient Israel and
Judaism as a legitimate inquiry into history. This is clearly evi-
denced by such prophets as Hosea (Hosea 12:10) and by the many
anecdotes and stories contained in the Talmud and other Jewish
writings. Recently the use of symbolism and typology to interpret
some of the enigmas of early Israelite ''myths'' into understandable ''historical sequences'' has been used rather extensively by
such scholars as G. Mendenhall, G. E. Wright, Umhau Wolf, W.
F. Albright, and John Bright.[11]

To interpret Jonah by using a typological, symbolical, or foreshadowing method should thus be not only acceptable but necessary if one is seeking to understand the full implications of the
book and its message.

Joseph Campbell and Mircea Eliade have both made considerable contributions to the study of symbolism and typologies by
intense scrutiny of the literature they label ''myths'' and ''hero
stories.''

Eliade says: ''Myth means a 'true story' . . . [which] is always
an account of a creation; it relates how something was produced,
began to be. Myth tells only of that which *really* happened, which
manifested itself completely.''[12] He then outlines five criteria for
the ''structure and function'' of myths:

1. [Myth] constitutes the History of the acts of the Supernaturals. . . .
2. This History is considered to be absolutely true (because it is concerned with realities) and sacred (because it is the work of the Supernaturals). . . .
3. Myth is always related to a "creation," it tells how something came into existence, or how a pattern of behavior, an institution, a manner of working were established; this is why myths constitute the paradigms for all significant human acts. . . .
4. By knowing the myth one knows the "origin" of things and hence can control and manipulate them at will; this is not an "external," "abstract" knowledge but a knowledge that one "experiences" ritually, either by ceremonially recounting the myth or by performing the ritual for which it is the justification. . . .
5. In one way or another one "lives" the myth, in the sense that one is seized by the sacred, exalting power of the events recollected or re-enacted.[13]

For Eliade, "myths," or the things that really happen, are the most true and the most real of all events and must be experienced by man; they must also assist him in coming to "God." This is most often, but not always, attained by making myths into repeatable rituals; it may be attained by the use of an intense means of recall.

Campbell suggests the following:

The standard path of the mythological adventure of the hero is a magnification of the formula represented in the rites of passage: [as outlined by Eliade] *separation—initiation—return:* which might be named the nuclear unit of the monomyth. *A hero ventures forth from the world of common day into a region of supernatural wonder: fabulous forces are there encountered and a decisive victory is won: the hero comes back from this mysterious adventure with·the power to bestow boons on his fellow man.*[14]

Campbell further breaks down the three parts of the "nuclear unit" of the monomyth. The first part, "Separation from the World," includes five major points:
1. The Call to Adventure or the Herald
2. Refusal of the Call—or folly of the flight from God

3. Supernatural Aid—benign, protecting, power of destiny
4. Crossing the first threshold—Guards—bestowers of "magic" power
5. Whale's Belly—Death

Each of the other two parts is divided into six points, some of which are "Rescue from Without," "Master of Two Worlds," and "Freedom to *Live* or Resurrection and Rebirth."[15]

When the history of Jonah is considered in the context of symbolic interpretation and measured against Eliade's criteria for a "true myth," it fulfills all the requirements of a "true story" or "myth" which "really" happened. *Its importance is in telling how the spiritual principles of repentance and resurrection work and how to control and manipulate them.*

When Jonah is analyzed using Campbell's criteria for the adventure of the "hero," it also correlates with great precision. For example, Campbell's "call to adventure" is fulfilled in Jonah 1:1-2 when the Lord calls Jonah to go to Nineveh. The "refusal of the call" is most obvious when he flees physically by the ship from Joppa, and spiritually by sleeping in the hold of the ship (Jonah 1:3-5). "Supernatural aid" of the "benign" nature is given by the steersman, the lots, and "the rowing hard for shore" (Jonah 1:6-9). Jonah "crosses the first threshold" through great danger when he is finally thrown into the sea by the crew (Jonah 1:11-15). Finally, in his "separation from the world" Jonah enters the "whale's belly" or death in *dag gadol,* the "great fish" (Jonah 2:1). Campbell says:

> This popular motif [the whale's belly] gives emphasis to the lesson that the passage of the threshold is a form of self-annihilation . . . the hero goes inward, to be born again. The disappearance corresponds to the passing of a worshiper into a temple—where he is to be quickened by the recollection of who and what he is, namely dust and ashes, unless immortal. The temple interior, the belly of the whale, and the heavenly land beyond, above, and below the confines of the world are one and the same.[16]

Each of the other two parts of the monomyth matches up with similar detail. Jonah is the epitome of Campbell's "adventurous mythological hero."

Both Eliade and Campbell stress that "myths" which match the patterns just outlined are concerned with the means by which a man experiences a "new birth"—the old man dies; a new man is born.

Erwin Goodenough[17] has also discussed the symbolic value of the fish in Judaism, trying to show its origins and uses. He says the fish is the pious student, the Messiah, sacramental or eucharistic food, a sign of fertility, and finally a symbol of the hope of immortality. It is in this final category that he places the fish in the story of Jonah:

> It is quite possible that a Jewish Jonah existed in art as an antetype to the Jonah so early and commonly found on Christian graves. Indeed one amulet [previously thought to be Christian] . . . seems more probably Jewish . . . [with] this value of giving immortality.[18]

The three days and three nights Jonah was in the belly of the fish, followed by his release, was a very old Jewish tradition and "symbolized the resurrection from the dead . . . which Christians took over for Jesus."[19]

Goodenough also briefly interpreted the "elaborately allegorized" recounting of the story of Jonah recorded in the *Zohar:* "[It] has preserved from the early period much of the Judaism of nonrabbinic Jews."[20] In this particular case it contains material which was also compatible with at least some of the rabbinic material. Though the *Zohar* is a very late work, it must at least be recognized as an authentic tradition carrier from much earlier times.[21] As the account in the *Zohar* is rather long, only some of the salient points will be identified.

> In the story of Jonah we have a representation of the whole of man's career in this world. Jonah descending into the ship is symbolic of man's soul that descends into this world to enter into his body. . . . Man, then, is in this world as in a ship that is traversing the great ocean and is like to be broken, as it says, "so that the ship was like to be broken"(Jonah 1, 4). Furthermore, man in this world commits sins, imagining that he can flee from the presence of his Master, who takes no notice for this world. . . . It is [man's doom] which assails the ship and calls to mind man's sins that it may seize him; and the man is thus caught by the tempest and is struck down by illness, just as Jonah "went down into the innermost part of the ship; and he lay, and was fast asleep. Although the man is thus prostrated, his soul does not exert itself to return to his Master in order to make good his omissions. So "The shipmaster came to him," to

wit, the good prompter, who is the general steersman, "and said unto him: What meanest thou that thou sleepest? Arise, call upon thy God," etc.; it is not a time to sleep, as they are about to take thee up to be tried for all that thou hast done in this world. Repent of thy sins. Reflect on these things and return to thy Master. . . . They bring him to judgment before the Heavenly Tribunal that tempest, that is none other than the judgment doom which raged against him, demands from the King the punishment of all the King's prisoners, and then all the King's counsellors appear before Him one by one, and the Tribunal is set up. Should the man be found guilty, as in the case of Jonah, then "the men rowed hard to bring it to the land, but they could not"; find points in his favour and strive to restore him to this world, but they cannot; "for prosecution storms and rages against him, and, convicting him of his sins, prevails against his defenders. . . . Regarding such a man it is written, "and they cast him forth into the sea, and the sea ceased from its raging," that is, only after they have placed him in the grave, which is the raging. For the fish that swallowed him is, in fact, the grave; and so "Jonah was in the belly of the fish," which is identified with "the belly of the underworld" *(Sheol),* as is proved by the passage, "Out of the belly of the underworld *(Sheol)* cried I." "Three days and three nights.". . . After that the soul ascends whilst the body is being decomposed in the earth, where it will lie until the time when the Holy One, blessed be He, will awaken the dead. A voice will then resound through the graves, proclaiming: "Awake and sing, ye that dwell in the dust, for thy dew is as the dew of light, and the earth shall cast forth the dead *(rephaim)*" (Isaiah 19). That will come to pass when the Angel of Death will depart from the world, as it is written: "He will destroy death forever, and the Lord God will wipe away tears from off all faces; and the reproach of his people will he take away from all the earth" (Isaiah 25:8). It is of that occasion that it is written: "And the Lord spoke unto the fish, and it vomited out Jonah upon the dry land"; for as soon as that voice will resound among the graves they will all cast out the dead bodies that they contain. . . . Thus in the narrative of that fish we find words of healing for the whole earth. As soon as it swallowed Jonah it died, but after three days was restored to life and vomited him forth. In a similar way the Land of Israel will in the future first be stirred to new life, and afterwards "the earth will cast forth the dead."[22]

Though the *Zohar* is quite late, the ideas and conceptions in it are important. In summary, the ship represents the body, and as Jonah entered into the ship, so an individual would enter into a physical body upon this earth. A tempest arises. That tempest is the judgment bar; it is the summons to come to the heavenly judgment to find out whether the price has been paid. Jonah being asleep is likened to a man being spiritually asleep, not paying attention to the Spirit or to the direction in which he should be going. The good prompter, the steersman or the master of the ship, must awaken him. The sea is the grave, the place of judgment. The fish is the grave and death. In other words, as Jonah is swallowed by the fish he dies physically and is in danger of dying spiritually. Finally, his being cast up or regurgitated by the fish symbolizes his rebirth or his "resurrection," not resurrection in the final sense as we would identify it but resurrection in the context of a new chance at life. This typological interpretation can easily be that of a literal historical prophet who lived his life as an example, testimony, or foreshadowing of the power of the resurrection by the Lord and the regenerative power of repentance. There is no doubt that ancient Judaism and probably ancient Israel believed that the story of Jonah was a story of a literal prophet who was swallowed by a great fish. When this prophet died in the belly of that fish, his spirit had the opportunity of being taught and trained and then brought back to life to testify of the atoning power of the God of Israel. The Savior saw, understood, and effectively likened the "sign of Jonah" to himself. As Jonah came forth from "death," so also would the Messiah.

The experience of Jonah's "death and rebirth" is not altogether unique for Latter-day Saints, as shown by the story Alma recounted to his son Helaman.

> And now, O my son Helaman, behold, thou art in thy youth, and therefore, I beseech of thee that thou wilt hear my words and learn of me; for I do know that whosoever shall put their trust in God shall be supported in all their trials, and their troubles, and their afflictions, and shall be lifted up at the last day.
>
> And I would not that ye think that I know of myself—not of the temporal but of the spiritual, not of the carnal mind but of God.
>
> Now, behold, I say unto you, if I had not been born of God I should not have known these things; but God has, by the mouth of his holy angel, made these things known unto me, not of any worthiness of myself.

For I went about with the sons of Mosiah, seeking to destroy the church of God; but behold, God sent his holy angel to stop us by the way.

And behold, he spake unto us, as it were the voice of thunder, and the whole earth did tremble beneath our feet; and we all fell to the earth, for the fear of the Lord came upon us.

But behold, the voice said unto me: Arise. And I arose and stood up and beheld the Angel.

And he said unto me: If thou wilt of thyself be destroyed, seek no more to destroy the church of God.

And it came to pass that I fell to the earth; and it was for the space of three days and three nights that I could not open my mouth, neither had I the use of my mouth, neither had I the use of my limbs.

And the angel spake more things unto me, which were heard by my brethren, but I did not hear them; for when I heard the words—If thou wilt be destroyed of thyself, seek no more to destroy the church of God—I was struck with such great fear and amazement lest perhaps I should be destroyed that I fell to the earth and I did hear no more.

But I was racked with eternal torment, for my soul was harrowed up to the greatest degree and racked with all my sins.

Yea, I did remember all my sins and iniquities, for which I was tormented with the pains of hell; yea, I saw that I had rebelled against my God, and that I had not kept his holy commandments.

Yea, and I had murdered many of his children, or rather led them away unto destruction; yea, and in fine so great had been my iniquities, that the very thought of coming into the presence of my God did rack my soul with inexpressible horror.

Oh, thought I, that I could be banished and become extinct both soul and body, that I might not be brought to stand in the presence of my God, to be judged of my deeds.

And now, for three days and for three nights was I racked, even with the pains of a damned soul.

And it came to pass that as I was thus racked with torment, while I was harrowed up by the memory of my many sins, behold, I remembered also to have heard my father prophesy unto the people concerning the coming of one Jesus Christ, a Son of God, to atone for the sins of the world.

Now, as my mind caught hold upon this thought, I cried within my heart: O Jesus, thou Son of God, have mercy on me, who am in the gall of bitterness, and am encircled about by the everlasting chains of death.

And now, behold, when I thought this, I could remember my pains no more; yea, I was harrowed up by the memory of my sins no more.

And oh, what joy, and what marvelous light I did behold; yea, my world was filled with joy as exceeding as was my pain! . . .

Yea, methought I saw, even as our father Lehi saw, God sitting upon his throne, surrounded with numberless concourses of angels, in the attitude of singing and praising their God; yea, and my soul did long to be there.

But behold, my limbs did receive their strength again, and I stood upon my feet, and did manifest unto the people that I had been born of God.

Yea, and from that time even until now, I have labored without ceasing, that I might bring souls unto repentance; that I might bring them to taste of the exceeding joy which I did taste; that they might also be born of God, and be filled with the Holy Ghost. . . .

And I know that he will raise me up at the last day, to dwell with him in glory; yea, and I will praise him forever, for he has brought our fathers out of Egypt, and he has swallowed up the Egyptians in the Red Sea; and he led them by his power into the promised land; yea, and he has delivered them out of bondage and captivity from time to time.

Yea, and he has also brought our fathers out of the land of Jerusalem; and he has also, by his everlasting power, delivered them out of bondage and captivity, from time to time even down to the present day; and I have always retained in remembrance their captivity; yea, and ye also ought to retain in remembrance, as I have done, their captivity.

But behold, my son, this is not all; for ye ought to know as I do know, that inasmuch as ye shall keep the commandments of God ye shall prosper in the land; and ye ought to know also, that inasmuch as ye will not keep the commandments of God ye shall be cut off from his presence. Now this is according to his word. (Alma 36:3-20, 22-24, 28-30.)

Alma also testified in Mosiah 27:29-30:

My soul hath been redeemed from the gall of bitterness and bonds of iniquity. I was in the darkest abyss; but now I behold the marvelous light of God. My soul was racked with eternal torment; but I am snatched, and my soul is pained no more.

I rejected my Redeemer, and denied that which had been spoken of by our fathers; but now that they may foresee that he will come, and that he remembereth every creature of his creating, he will make himself manifest unto all.

The parallels between the stories of Jonah and Alma are stunning. Both men disregarded God as an effective force in their lives (see Alma 36:6; Jonah 1:3, 6). Both refused to "save" the souls of those they were called to serve. Both "died" and were "racked with eternal torment" in "hell." Both felt the "chains of the abyss" or "everlasting death" weighing them down. Both finally turned to the Savior, remembering his power to atone for the sins of mankind. Both became diligent servants for their God, testifying of the importance of repentance and the effective application of the Atonement in their lives and the lives of their "charges."

Jonah became a type to Israel and the Ninevites of (1) the literalness of the power of resurrection and (2) the need to take advantage of the Atonement through repentance if one desired full association with God in his presence. For Alma the emphasis lay with the latter principle, the need to take advantage of the Atonement through repentance, though he too was "snatched" from the awful "abyss" where he had been encircled with "everlasting chains of death."

Jonah chapter 4 gives us a further key to understanding the relationship between repentance and the Atonement in his message. The power to live is a gift of God, just as the protecting *kikion* was a gift. As Jonah had little to do with the growth of the plant, so we have relatively little to do with our outward appearance. Yet it was not the appearance of the plant that held importance for Jonah; it was the internal "wholeness" of the plant that mattered. Without the internal structure to drink the "living water" and thus sustain itself, the plant dried and withered when the sun came up. So it would appear to be the case for those who cannot spiritually drink of the "living water" because they are corrupted internally. When the "Son" comes, they "that do wickedly shall be as stubble; and I will burn them up, saith the Lord of Hosts, that wickedness shall not be upon the earth" (D&C 29:9). To enjoy a full life with God, to be resurrected in glory, one must be internally whole. That can occur only if the Atonement is brought to bear upon the lives of men. Jonah testifies that only through the atonement of the God of Israel can both the physical and spiritual rebirth of man take place. Jonah is therefore not merely a "myth," an "adventurous hero" or even a man "kept alive." Jonah is the sign of the relationship of the Atonement to the power of repentance and the resurrection of all mankind. "And there shall be no sign [given] . . . but the sign of the prophet

Jonah: for as Jonah was three days and three nights in the whale's belly; so shall the Son of man be three days and three nights in the heart of the earth. The men of Nineveh shall rise in judgment with this generation, and shall condemn it; because they repented at the preaching of Jonah; and, behold, a greater than Jonah is here." (Matthew 12:39-41.)

Notes

1. The word "with" in the last sentence would be better translated "against." The translations used in this paper are from *The Holy Bible: King James Version,* C Series (New York: American Bible Society, 1971), and *The New English Bible* (Oxford: Oxford University Press, 1970). Those of the author are taken from *Biblia Hebraica,* ed. R. Kittel.

2. H. G. Liddell and Robert Scott, *A Greek-English Lexicon* (New York: Harper and Brothers, 1861), p. 432. The original Greek term means "any sea monster or huge fish, [Homer, Herodotus II] an abyss, hollow."

3. Robert H. Pfeiffer, *The Books of the Old Testament* (New York: Harper and Row, Harper Chapel Books, 1957), p. 306.

4. Edward J. Young, *An Introduction to the Old Testament* (Grand Rapids, Mich.: William B. Eerdman's Publishing Co., 1965), p. 262.

5. Otto Eissfeldt, *The Old Testament: An Introduction,* trans. Peter R. Ackroyd (New York: Harper and Row, 1966); James King West, *Introduction to the Old Testament: Hear O Israel* (New York: Macmillan, 1971), pp. 376-77.

6. For an example of this see W. Cleon Skousen, *The Fourth Thousand Years* (Salt Lake City: Bookcraft, 1966), pp. 458-64.

7. See Yohanan Aharoni and Michael Avi-Yonah, *The Macmillan Bible Atlas* (New York: Macmillan, 1973), map 117 (p. 75).

8. J. H. Hertz, *The Pentateuch and Haftorahs,* 5 vols. (London: Oxford University Press, 1951), 1:318. In Francis Brown, S. R. Driver, and Charles A. Briggs, *Hebrew and English Lexicon of the Old Testament* (London: Oxford Clarendon Press, 1907; hereafter referred to as BDB), pp. 982-83, *Sheol* is defined as "the underworld . . . whither men descend at death"; it is a place of "judgment." There the "condition" of the righteous and the wicked is distinguished. To the wicked it becomes a place of dire straits, but to the righteous it becomes a refinement. (See Genesis 37:35; 42:30; 44:29, 31; 1 Samuel 2:6; 28; 1 Kings 2:6-9; Isaiah 14:11-15; Psalm 88:4; Numbers 16:30-33; Job 17:16.) Without the Atonement no one would have escaped death and the grave of *Sheol.* (See Psalms 30:4; 86:13; 16:10.)

9. BDB, p. 884. *Kikion* is more correctly translated as castor bean instead of gourd.

10. Umberto Cassuto, *Commentary on Exodus* (Jerusalem: Magnus Press, 1967), p. 15.

11. G. Mendenhall, "The Hebrew Conquest of Palestine," *Biblical Archaeologist* 25 (1962):66-87; G. E. Wright, "The Literary and Historical Problem of Joshua 10 and Judges 1," *Journal of Near Eastern Studies* 5 (1946): 105-15; Umhau Wolf, "Terminology of Israel's Tribal Organization," *Journal of Biblical Literature* 75 (1946):45-49; W. F. Albright, "The Israelite Conquer of Canaan in the Light of Archaeology," *Bulletin of American Schools of Oriental Research* 74 (1939):11-23; John Bright, *History of Israel* (Philadelphia: Westminster Press, 1959).

12. Mircea Eliade, *Myth and Reality,* trans. Willard R. Trask (New York and Evanston: Harper Torch Books, 1968), p. 6.

13. Ibid., pp. 18-19.

14. Joseph Campbell, *The Hero with a Thousand Faces* (Cleveland and New York: World Publishing Co., Meridian Books, 1969), p. 30.

15. Ibid., pp. 207, 229, 238, 245.

16. Ibid., pp. 91-92.

17. Erwin Goodenough, *Jewish Symbols in the Greco-Roman Period,* vol. 5 (New York: Bollinger Foundation, 1956), p. 6.

18. Ibid., p. 48.

19. Ibid., p. 48.

20. Ibid., p. 47.

21. Louis Ginzberg, *On Jewish Law and Lore* (New York: Atheneum, A Temple Book, 1977), esp. "The Significance of the Halachah for Jewish History" and "Allegorical Interpretation of Scripture." Compare Gershom Scholem, *On the Kabbalah and Its Symbolism* (New York: Schocken Books, 1969), esp. "Kabbalah and Myth."

22. Harvey Sperling and Maurice Simon, *The Zohar,* vol. 4 (New York: Rebeca Bennet Pub., 1958), pp. 173-76.

6

History and Jeremiah's Crisis of Faith

S. Kent Brown

Before we begin our review of the parts of Jeremiah's early ministry, let us first set out the usual and customary picture of it.[1] The prophet received his call while still a young man, during the thirteenth year of King Josiah's reign, about 627 or 626 B.C. In his early prophecies, he spoke of an unidentified peril which was to come upon Jerusalem and Judah from the north (see Jeremiah 1:13-16; 4:6; 6:1). Until about seventy years ago,[2] virtually all scholars believed that this was a reference to the Scythian hordes which swept through Syria and Palestine on their way to and from Egypt, and of which only the Greek historian Herodotus had something to say.[3] If indeed the Scythians were the peril envisioned by Jeremiah, then his predictions about Jerusalem's destruction by that foe remained unfulfilled. I wish to note here, parenthetically, that I do not personally believe that this unidentified evil at the time of the prophet's early ministry was the Scythian army. But more on this later. When this prophecy was not shortly fulfilled, Jeremiah lapsed into a period of silence. That the prophet was deeply troubled by the apparent nonfulfillment of his prophecies we learn from the so-called Confessions of Jeremiah (usually considered to be six in number: see Jeremiah 11:18-12:6; 15:10-21; 17:9-10, 14-18; 18:18-23; 20:7-12; 20:14-18). It is worth recalling, additionally, that 621 B.C. saw the discovery of the Book of the Law in the temple, upon which King Josiah based an extensive religious

reform (2 Kings 22:8)[4] To all appearances, Jeremiah enthusiasti-
cally supported this revision, which both initially did away with all
of the small shrines, whether dedicated to *YHWH* or to other non-
Israelite deities, and attempted to centralize sacrificial worship at
Jerusalem.[5] This reformation must have had a debilitating impact
on the livelihood of Jeremiah's priestly family, who not only lived
in Anathoth but also probably officiated at one of the local discon-
tinued shrines, thus explaining in part their strong opposition to
his ministry.[6] When the strength and purpose of the reform began
to wane, Jeremiah withdrew his endorsement.[7] Then, when
Jehoiakim came to the throne after Josiah's untimely death, the
prophet once again took up his predictions concerning the peril
from the north, this time applying them to the Chaldeans, who had
newly arisen as an international power.

Every detail of this brief traditional outline of Jeremiah's early
ministry has been challenged.[8] For instance, concerning the relationship between the Scythian incursion and the prophet's despair
—the major items which will hold our attention here—no less a
scholar than Professor John Bright wrote in 1959 that Herodotus's
assertion that "the Scythians . . . ran wild over western Asia,
ranging as far as the Egyptian frontier, is to be received with greatest caution; though some scholars accept it and explain the oracles
of Zephaniah and young Jeremiah in light of it, it is quite without
objective support.''[9] Bright here dismisses Herodotus's account
without discussion. Bearing in mind the need to consider later the
validity of Herodotus's witness, let us first turn to the problem of
the identification of the foe from the north, the solution to which
will have to take into account the Greek historian.

At the time of his call, Jeremiah saw two visions (see Jeremiah
1:11, 13),[10] the second of which included a view of "a seething
pot" boiling in the north. Its contents were to be poured out on
Jerusalem and the land of Judah, for, as the Lord said: "Out of
the north an evil shall break forth upon all the inhabitants of the
land. For, lo, I will call all the families of the kingdoms of the
north, saith the Lord; and they shall come, and they shall set every
one his throne at the entering of the gates of Jerusalem, and
against all the walls thereof round about, and against all the cities
of Judah. And I will utter my judgments against them touching all
their wickedness." (Jeremiah 1:14-16a.) This picture of wide-

spread destruction and punishment from the north became a feature of Jeremiah's message from the opening of his ministry.[11] Notably, in each reference to this peril (see Jeremiah 1:14ff.; 4:6;
6:1), just who was coming from the north remained unknown, apparently even to the prophet, for it was not until a much later date
in his ministry that he identified this punishing force as the Chaldeans from Babylonia (see Jeremiah 21:4, 9; 22:25). We can observe thus far, then, that the Lord had apparently revealed to the
youthful Jeremiah only the northerly route by which the peril
would travel to Palestine,[12] but not the foe who would come.

We noted earlier that something had occurred during the early
years of the prophet's career which drove him to complain bitterly
about unfulfilled prophecies. Among other things, the situation
had resulted in Jeremiah's being totally and publicly discredited.
In fact, even his family had joined in a plot to take his life, apparently because whatever had happened had created an enormous
public outcry against him. What had occurred that caused the
prophet to complain so and motivated his family and friends to
seek his life? It does not seem possible that Jeremiah's open
support of Josiah's religious reforms would have generated such a
furor—even if those revisions eventually lost popular support, as
some scholars maintain.[13] After all, Josiah was still living at the
time.[14] We must seek a better explanation. And the only other
possible and feasible solution is the Scythian hypothesis.

Herodotus says that the Scythians, after becoming masters of
Asia, marched south intending to invade Egypt.[15] En route they
passed along the coastline of Syria and Palestine, a movement
which surely was known to the inhabitants of Judah and would
have spread alarm. Arriving at the border of Egypt, between the
Philistine kingdom and the Delta region, the Scythians were met
by Pharaoh Psammeticus and were bribed with gifts and per-
suaded not to invade the Nile Valley. The Scythians then retraced
their steps, plundering at least the Philistine city of Ashkelon.
Incidentally, this second sweep past the outlying communities of
Judah would also have been known in Jerusalem. After returning
to Asia, the Scythians were said to have ruled for twenty-eight
years before their power waned.

Scholars have raised major objections against this narration by
Herodotus. The first concerns its historicity. The protests range

from outright denials of the incidents mentioned to an insistence
that Herodotus's information is questionable.[16] But no real foundation exists for rejecting his narrative out of hand. To be sure,
Herodotus's major interest centered on the possible relation of
Aphrodite to the goddess of Ashkelon, whose city was attacked.
But Herodotus's interest in Aphrodite does not call the historicity
of the entire incident into question. Neither is there any reason to
suppose that the priests at Ashkelon made up the story merely to
entertain inquisitive visitors to their city.[17] Moreover, the fact that
the Bible makes no specific mention of this incident, and that it
was narrated by Herodotus alone, does not destroy his credibility
in the least.[18] On the contrary, his trustworthiness as a reliable
source is buttressed by two pieces of evidence. The first is the
existence of Jeremiah's confessions, written in the wake of a crisis
which caused the prophet deep personal disappointment, coupled
with the resulting public outcry against him. Clearly, some major
external event had happened to bring about this circumstance.
Admittedly, I am here engaging a bit in circular reasoning by
saying, on the one hand, that if the Scythians came Jeremiah's
situation can be explained and, on the other, that if the prophet's
circumstance is to be rightly understood then we shall likely see
the Scythian incursion lying behind it. For good or bad, this is
often how one has to deal with historical connections which on the
surface are not readily apparent. But there is more. The second
piece of evidence stems from the existence of the name
Scythopolis, a toponym associated with an ancient city which lay
in the Jordan Valley a few miles south of the Sea of Galilee. The
origin of this name has puzzled investigators. The town was originally called Bethshan, mentioned as early as Joshua 17:11 as
belonging to the tribe of Manasseh.[19] At a date prior to the second
century B.C., this city acquired the name Scythopolis[20] and was
reckoned within the Decapolis district, which was made up of ten
non-Jewish cities in the regions of Galilee and Gilead.[21] Several
hypotheses have been proposed to explain the genesis of the
toponym Scythopolis, including Jerome's which suggested that the
proximity of the biblical town Sukkoth (Genesis 33:17), whose
consonants are s-k-t, had given Bethshan its new name. But the
most natural explanation is that some of the Scythian band who
had gone to the border of Egypt did not return with the main body

to Asia. Instead, they turned aside when they came to Galilee and settled in the area near Bethshan. Eventually, in this view, it was these people who gave the town its name in the Greek period as a result of waning Israelite influences during and after the exile in Babylon.[22]

The second major problem facing the Scythian hypothesis consists in dating their incursion. If they came at a time removed from Jeremiah's early ministry, the hypothesis does not hold. Let us state what is securely known. First of all, the Scythians came during the reign of Pharaoh Psammeticus (who died 610 B.C.). Secondly, the invasion occurred before the destruction of Nineveh by Cyaxares the Mede in 612 B.C.[23] Further, Egypt went to the aid of the crumbling Assyrian empire in 616 B.C.,[24] the earliest *terminus ante quem* we can firmly establish. Scholars such as H. H. Rowley have suggested that the incursion likely occurred even before this, perhaps prior to 621 B.C., the beginning of Josiah's reform.[25] Whether or not this idea holds, we can safely say—based simply on what can be demonstrated historically—that the crisis which precipitated Jeremiah's troubles fell before 616 B.C., within a decade of his call. Such a conclusion supports the observations of others that the renewal of Jeremiah's call, which appears at the end of his second confession in chapter 15, verses 20 and 21, must have followed a major setback early in his ministry rather than late.[26]

Having now established the high probability, not only that Herodotus's record of the Scythian invasion is historically reliable, but also that this invasion came within the first years of Jeremiah's ministry, we turn to the confessions themselves. Taken together,[27] the confessions clearly demonstrate both that the prophet was deeply disappointed because of unfulfilled prophecies and that, consequently, he felt God had abandoned him. In these solemn dirges one plainly sees that Jeremiah passed through a crisis which shook his faith in the Lord. Let us first discuss the confessions in order (see Jeremiah 11:18-12:6; 15:10-21; 17:9f., 14-18; 18:18-23; 20:7-12, 14-18),[28] and then suggest a reconstruction of events which led to his difficulties.

The first passage brings chapter 11 to a close and opens chapter 12 (see Jeremiah 11:18-12:6). Jeremiah recorded here that the Lord had revealed to him a plot against his life hatched by "the men of Anathoth" (Jeremiah 11:21), his hometown (see Jeremiah 1:1). In this connection, Jeremiah noted that the instigators of the plot went so far as to speak in riddles when discussing his planned murder in his presence (see Jeremiah 11:19). His narrow escape from death seemingly led him to ask, "Wherefore doth the way of the wicked prosper? Wherefore are all they happy that deal very treacherously? Thou hast planted them, yea, they have taken root: they grow, yea, they bring forth fruit; thou art near in their mouth and far from their reins." (Jeremiah 12:1f.)[29] What the prophet said next forms an important key to understanding his own tortured frustrations and disappointments. "Thou, O Lord, knowest me: thou hast seen me, and tried mine heart toward thee" (Jeremiah 12:3). Note the theme of trial, a concept which we shall stress again. The prophet has here claimed for the first time that the Lord had "tried" his loyalty. He continued by pleading that the Lord avenge him against his enemies. Then the Lord gently reprimanded him (see Jeremiah 12:5f.): "If thou hast run with the footmen, and they have wearied thee, then how canst thou contend with horses? And if in the land of peace, wherein thou trustedst, they wearied thee, then how wilt thou do in the swelling of Jordan?" God's message to the prophet was plain—matters were only to become worse. The Lord went on to say, "For even thy brethren, and the house of thy father, even they have dealt treacherously with thee; yea, they have called a multitude after thee: believe them not, though they speak fair words unto thee" (Jeremiah 12:6). Whatever had happened, it is clear that it had turned not only the people in Jeremiah's hometown but even members of his own family against him. In fact, the anger had run so deeply among family members that they too had participated in the plot against his life.

The second of the six confessions occurs in chapter 15. The prophet began it by saying, "Woe is me, my mother, that thou hast borne me a man of strife and a man of contention to the whole earth!" (Jeremiah 15:10.) He then sorrowed that, although he had neither lent nor borrowed, everyone hated him. After he next quoted the Lord's words concerning the fate of himself and of a remnant of Judah to be spared destruction,[30] Jeremiah continued:

> O Lord, thou knowest: remember me, and visit me, and revenge me of my persecutors; take me not away in thy long-

suffering: know that for thy sake I have suffered rebuke. (Jeremiah 15:15.)

It is absolutely clear both from this and from earlier passages that he had suffered severe persecution. And we know that some of it came from his family and old associates in Anathoth. Listen now to his following words as he reflected on his call:

Thy words were found, and I did eat them, thy word was unto me the joy and rejoicing of mine heart: for I am called by thy name, O Lord, God of hosts. (Jeremiah 15:16.)

One can imagine Jeremiah remembering the joy and happiness which came to him when he was first called to be a spokesman to God's people. But after mentioning that this event effectively set him apart from others (see Jeremiah 15:17), he wrote a gloomy confession of his frustrations since his call:

Why is my pain perpetual, and my wound incurable, which refuseth to be healed? Wilt thou be altogether unto me as a liar, and as waters that fail? (Jeremiah 15:18.)

Here, mentioning his injury which seemingly could not be healed, Jeremiah dared to refer to God as "failing waters."[31] In a word, the prophet was distressed. What had gone wrong? Significantly, this outburst led the Lord generously to reconfirm Jeremiah's prophetic calling, almost—as we noted earlier—in the very words of his original commission (see Jeremiah 15:20-21; cf. 1:17-19).

In his third confession, appearing in chapter 17, Jeremiah again stated that the Lord had been trying him severely. He quoted the Lord as saying, "I the Lord search the heart, I try the reins, even to give every man according to his ways, and according to the fruit of his doings" (Jeremiah 17:10). But even though he had been severely tested, the prophet acknowledged that only the Lord finally could help him (see Jeremiah 17:14).

Verse 15 may hold a clue as to what had happened. We read: "Behold, they say unto me, where is the word of the Lord? Let it come now." Plainly, Jeremiah was being teased and ridiculed because what he had prophesied had not come about. Something had obviously gone amiss—at least in the view of his hearers—and he was being baited to say more and thus compound his apparent errors. In this connection, we observe that in his fourth confession (see Jeremiah 18:18-23) he noted how his persecutors devised ways to trap him in his words so that they might refute him and not feel obliged to listen seriously to his message. Again, it is worthwhile to point out the prophet's reference here to constant harassment and persecution.

Jeremiah's fifth confession (Jeremiah 20:7-12) contains what is perhaps his most poignant statement:

> O Lord, thou hast deceived me, and I was deceived: thou art stronger than I, and hast prevailed: I am in derision daily, everyone mocketh me. (Jeremiah 20:7.)

He went on to say that his trust in the word of the Lord had fallen so low that he had decided to quit,[32] not to "speak any more in his name, But his word was in my heart as a burning fire shut up in my bones, and I was weary with forbearing, and I could not stay" from uttering the words of the Lord. (Jeremiah 20:9.) The feeling that he was deceived finds close links with the theme of trial when, almost immediately afterward, he mentioned the "Lord of hosts, that triest the righteous" (Jeremiah 20:12). So intense had persecution of him become that Jeremiah, who once had prayed for his people, now demanded that the Lord take vengeance on those who treated him despitefully.

The last confession (Jeremiah 20:14-18) was written in the depths of despair. I know of only one other mournful passage in all of scripture that can match its majestic blackness and sorrow.[33] Indeed, the prophet had been brought to the end of his strength and wit. His faith had run out. What made him feel that he had been deceived by God himself, that somehow the Lord had made sport of him and finally had abandoned him?

The answer, as I have suggested, is to be connected with the sudden appearance and then abrupt disappearance of the Scythians—tiny events when viewed against the massive events of the fall of the Assyrian Empire. But before I offer my final solution to the problem, I must briefly return to an issue discussed earlier in another context. It concerns the series of statements about an "evil from the north" (see Jeremiah 4:6), the instrument of God's wrath against the unrepentant kingdom of Judah. As we already noted, the identity of this peril was not known to Jeremiah during the early years of his ministry. We should now further observe that Zephaniah, whose ministry preceded that of Jeremiah by a few years, also knew of a peril that was to come out of the north.[34] Since Zephaniah did not name this foe in his writings, it is clear that Jeremiah could not have learned its identity from this source.

From our vantage point, we know the identity of that peril who the Lord said would come to destroy Jerusalem and its temple. It was, of course, the Babylonian army. Indeed, as we have seen, Jeremiah came to know in the latter part of his ministry that it was the Chaldeans who were the "evil [that] shall break forth upon all the inhabitants of the land" (Jeremiah 1:14; see 21:4, 9; 22:25). Let us bear this in mind as we review a series of events associated with the Assyrian Empire before and during Jeremiah's ministry.

In 721 B.C. Samaria, then the capital of the kingdom of Israel, fell to the Assyrians after a three-year siege led by Shalmeneser V (727-722 B.C.) and Sargon II (722-705 B.C.) (see 2 Kings 17:5 ff.). We mark in passing Sargon's claim that he deported a total of 27,290 people.[35] By 664 B.C., just fifty-seven years after the fall of Samaria, Assyrian power and territory had reached their zenith. But this did not last long. In October 626 B.C., about the time of Jeremiah's call, the Babylonian prince Nabopolassar defeated the Assyrians at Babylon, thus leading a successful revolt. Ten years later, the situation had become so desperate for Assyria that Egypt, an old nemesis and tribute-paying state, went to their assistance. Two years later, in 614 B.C., the capital city of Asshur was taken by Cyaxares, commander of the Medes. In 612 B.C., Nineveh itself fell to him while he was leading an allied force consisting of Medes, Babylonians, and possibly Scythian horsemen.[36] It was the Scythians who had earlier swept down from the southern marches of the present-day Soviet Union who draw our attention.

We now must review the events that, although seemingly insignificant on the larger Near Eastern stage, affected the early ministry of Jeremiah so deeply. From all we can learn, the Lord did not reveal the identity of the foe from the north either to Jeremiah, the young prophet from Anathoth, or to Zephaniah, who had prophesied of a similar peril. Bearing this in mind, we note that before Jeremiah had prophesied for a decade, regularly warning that such a foe would appear bringing death and destruction to the people of Judah, the Scythians had passed along the coast of Palestine. They were on their way to Egypt, looting and burning as they went.[37] The natural response of everyone in

Judah, apparently including the prophet, would have been to consider the appearance of the Scythians as the fulfillment of his prophecies. At that moment, then, when the Scythians came sweeping down the Mediterranean plain, word would have been quickly communicated to Jerusalem that an attack was imminent.

But the expected attack never came, The Scythians passed southward, doing no appreciable damage to Jewish settlements. Even on their return they made the city and temple of Ashkelon their main target, doing consequential damage to nothing else. Thus the Scythian threat came and went, and Jerusalem and the land of Judah remained untouched. What had appeared to be the impending fulfillment of Jeremiah's words simply evaporated. It was then that his credibility fell to an all-time low. Had not the threat vanished? Had not Jeremiah been proven a false prophet? In the resulting furor and embarrassment, the prophet grew inwardly puzzled, frustrated, and disappointed. For a time it must have appeared that the Lord had deceived him, and he became the laughingstock of everyone. It was at this point, I believe, that his family and friends sought to take away his life because he had brought upon them intolerable shame and embarrassment. The youth from Anathoth, who had seemingly succeeded in the highest possible way, had suddenly—to all appearances—proved to be false, both to his people and to his religion. To compound the public pain and humiliation of his family, he eventually continued his message of Judah's doom, at the Lord's behest, now, however, identifying the peril as the Chaldeans from Babylon.

It is to Jeremiah's everlasting credit that he remained faithful as he passed through an extraordinarily severe test of his trust in the Lord. But pass it he did. The most tragic of prophets, he emerged from this crucible of trial more deeply committed than ever. And he had to be so committed, for it was at least another thirty years before he saw the fulfillment of his woeful prophecies of destruction, the message which he had borne since the first of his career. Prophesying for more than four decades, he remained to the last of his ministry a lonely man speaking with a lonely voice in a sea of distrust, lack of faith, and sin. But in the end, God vindicated his servant's prophecies and thus his servant. This observation alone constitutes a message for our own day: God honors and supports his servants who are faithful.

Notes

1. A good summary of the range of problems concerning Jeremiah's early ministry is that by H. H. Rowley, "The Early Prophecies of Jeremiah in Their Setting," *Bulletin of the John Rylands Library* 45 (1962-63):198-234 (reprinted in Rowley's *Men of God* [1963], pp. 133-68). I am indebted to this insightful synopsis for much of my own understanding of this critical period in the prophet's career.

2. Rowley, pp. 206f. F. Wilke was among the first to reject the Scythian hypothesis: see *Alttestament-liche Studien, Rudolf Kittel zum 60. geburtstag dargebracht,* Beitrage zur Wissenschaft vom Alten Testament, vol. 13 (Leipzig: J. C. Hinrichs, 1913), pp. 222ff.

3. *The Histories,* I.104-6.

4. Almost without exception, scholars identify this Book of the Law as an early version of Deuteronomy. See Rowley's summarizing observation about this on pp. 226ff. A very extensive literature exists on this subject. Latter-day Saints, incidentally, should not be surprised at the assertion that Deuteronomy may have been known in varying versions, since, for example, what we read about Moses' end in Deuteronomy chapter 34 differs substantially from what must have been written on the brass plates, a notion based on the very different account of Moses' fate in Alma 45:19.

5. This is the usual reading of Jeremiah chapter 11, which, being full of Deuteronomic terminology and phraseology, apparently illustrates that Jeremiah was here advocating support of Josiah's reform. See Rowley, pp. 226f. for bibliography.

6. The notion that Jeremiah was an Aaronite priest descended from the high priest Abiathar, who was exiled by Solomon to Anathoth (1 Kings 2:26f.) has been challenged. To be sure, the phrase "of the priests" (Jeremiah 1:1) is omitted by the Septuagint. But there is no textual evidence against these words among Hebrew manuscripts (see Rowley, pp. 200, 203-6). One is always faced with the question of how to explain the opposition of the prophet's family. One logical answer, of course, is that the (Deuteronomic) reform somehow threatened their livelihood as priests of a local shrine. One notes that the name Anathoth derives from Anath, the name of a Canaanite goddess, possibly indicating that the town in pre-Israelite times housed a shrine dedicated to her. It would not be unusual for the Israelite priests to have taken over such a holy place and merely used it for their own worship. See the article on "Anathoth" in *The Interpreter's Dictionary of the Bible,* vol. 1 (Nashville: Abingdon, 1962), p. 125b.

7. This is the usual interpretation. But see the cautioning remarks of John Bright, *Jeremiah,* The Anchor Bible (Garden City, N.Y.: Doubleday, 1966), pp. xci-xcvi, 88f.

8. Rowley, pp. 199-201.

9. John Bright, *A History of Israel* (Philadelphia: Westminster, 1959), p. 293.

10. Questions have been raised whether the two visions accompanied Jeremiah's call (see Jeremiah 1:4-10). In *Jeremiah,* pp. 7f., Bright finally does admit that if they were not integral parts of Jeremiah's call they were given to him soon afterwards.

11. If one could demonstrate that Jeremiah's second vision (see Jeremiah 1:13ff.) came at a date significantly later than 627 or 626 B.C., the year of his call, then the vision could not have been (mistakenly) applied to the Scythians and would have referred from the first only to the Chaldeans. But nothing internal or external to the text supports a late date for this vision. See Bright, *Jeremiah,* pp. 7f.

12. Whether Jeremiah had the Scythians in mind, as some scholars maintain, or whether the Lord originally had reference to the Chaldeans, the route into Palestine for either would necessarily have been from the north. Rowley, pp. 214f.

13. Rowley, pp. 232-34.

14. The issue rests on the dating of the confessions. While it is rather certain that they were not all written at the same time (Rowley, pp. 220f.), their general date of composition is crucial if we are to place the prophet's crisis during Josiah's reign (640-609 B.C.), especially since the confessions relate the public and familial outcry against him (see Jeremiah 11:19-21; 12:6; 18:18, 22f.; 20:7f.; 10). One key is the second confession (see Jeremiah 15:10-21), which included a renewal of Jeremiah's call (vv. 20f.) in almost the same terms used in his initial summons by the Lord (cf. Jeremiah 1:18f.). As Rowley points out, the renewal "can most naturally be placed after his initial experience of failure," early in his ministry rather than late (p. 222). See John Bright, "A Prophet's Lament and Its Answer: Jeremiah 15:10-21," *Interpretation* 28 (1974):59-74.

15. Herodotus, *The Histories,* I.103-6.

16. See references in Rowley, pp. 208f.

17. Ibid., p. 209.

18. Ibid., pp. 211-12. A recently published review of the archaeological evidence which generally supports Herodotus's account is Edwin Yamauchi's "The Scythians: Invading Hordes from the Russian Steppes," *Biblical Archaeologist* 46 (Spring 1983):90-99. No less a scholar than T. R. Glover thought that Jeremiah had made clear reference to the Scythians in 6:22-23; see his *Herodotus,* Sather Classical Lectures (Berkeley: University of California Press, 1924), p. 95.

19. See also Judges 1:27; 1 Chronicles 7:29; and 1 Samuel 31:10, 12, where it is recorded that the bodies of Saul and Jonathan were hung on the wall of Bethshan by the Philistines. Josephus, in *Antiquities of the Jews* VI.xiv.8 [#374] and elsewhere, has noted that Scythopolis was the former Bethshan.

20. The Septuagint reading of Judges 1:27 makes the identification between Bethshan and Scythopolis. Hence, the latter would have been well established by the time of the translation of the book of Judges from Hebrew to Greek (third century or earlier?). That the new toponym was widely held by the second century B.C. can be seen by its appearance in 1 Maccabees 5:52; 7:36; and 2 Maccabees 12:39.

21. William Smith, ed., *Dictionary of Greek and Roman Geography,* vol. 1 (London: John Murray, 1873; reprint ed., AMS Press [1966]), pp. 398f., 757; Pauly-Wissowa, *Real-Encyclopadie der classischen Altertumswissenschaft,* Zweite Reihe [R-Z], Dritter Halbband, columns 947f.

22. Rowley, pp. 210f.

23. Herodotus, *The Histories,* I.103, 106.

24. See references in Rowley, pp. 202, 211.

25. Ibid., p. 211, makes the attractive suggestion that the prophetess Hulda was consulted about the Book of the Law (2 Kings 22:14ff.) because the young Jeremiah had already been discredited by this time, 621 B.C.

26. See note 14 above.

27. See Rowley's brief commentary, pp. 220-23. Bright has much more to say in his *Jeremiah.*

28. Recent studies include those by W. V. Chambers, "The Confessions of Jeremiah: A Study in Prophetic Ambivalence" (Ph.D. dissertation, Vanderbilt University, 1972); Cheng-Chang Wang, "A Theology of Frustration—An Interpretation of Jeremiah's Confessions," *South East Asia Journal of Theology,* 15 (1974):36-42; and P. Welten, "Leiden und Leidenserfahrung im Buch Jeremia," *Zeitschrift fur Theologie und Kirche* 74 (1977):123-50.

29. One hears echoes, of course, of a similar prayer uttered by the modern-day Prophet Joseph Smith in Liberty Jail (D&C 121:1-6). Compare Habakkuk 1:2-4, 13.

30. See the recent article on Jeremiah's citation of the words of the Lord here by G. V. Smith, "The Use of Quotations in Jeremiah XV 11-14," *Vetus Testamentum* 29 (1979):229-31.

31. Bright, *Jeremiah,* p. 110: "Literally 'a deceitful (brook),' a stream that goes dry in summer and cannot be depended upon for water. Remember that Jeremiah had once (see Jeremiah 2:13) called Yahweh 'the fountain of living waters'!"

32. The prophet's decision to remain silent has usually been associated with his disappointment in the reforms of Josiah (see Rowley, p. 200). But Jeremiah's words in chapter 20, verse 7, seem to point to a frustration growing out of something deeper. Consequently, I believe that his period of silence had to do with the seeming nonfulfillment of his prophecies, not with his disappointment in the reform movement. A treatment of all of chapter 20 appears in D. J. A. Clines, "Form, Occasion and Redaction in Jeremiah 20," *Zeitschrift fur die Alttestamentliche Wissenschaft* 88 (1976):390-409.

33. I refer to Job's lament (Job chapter 3).

34. Zephaniah 1:10 mentions a series of landmarks on the north side of Jerusalem past which the invaders were to come.

35. D. Winton Thomas, ed., *Documents from Old Testament Times* (reprint ed.; New York: Harper, 1961), pp. 58-63. A fuller range of texts appears in James

B. Pritchard, ed., *Ancient Near Eastern Texts*, 3d ed. with Supplement (Princeton: University Press, 1969), pp. 284-87.

36. See, for instance, A. Leo Oppenheim, *Ancient Mesopotamia: Portrait of a Dead Civilization* (Chicago: University of Chicago Press, 1964), pp. 161-63, 168-70; and Bright, *A History of Israel*, pp. 288-302.

37. It is Herodotus who mentioned the Scythian wont to plunder (*The Histories*, I.106).

7

Isaiah: Four Latter-day Keys to an Ancient Book

Avraham Gileadi

The book of Isaiah has effectively remained a "sealed book" until the last days because only in the last days have the means to its interpretation become available. On the one hand, the Book of Mormon alone brings together the keys essential to understanding Isaiah, while on the other, time itself sets the stage for Isaiah's prophecies to be fulfilled (cf. 2 Nephi 25:8). In the Book of Mormon, two keys for understanding Isaiah are given by Nephi and two by the Savior, though all overlap. The first two keys, which appear in 2 Nephi 25:4 and 5, may be defined respectively as the spirit and the letter of prophecy. The spirit of prophecy is spoken of as making "plain" the words of Isaiah, while the letter of prophecy causes one to "understand" them. The third and fourth keys, which appear in 3 Nephi 23:1 and 3, consist of the requirement to "search" the words of Isaiah in order to make meaningful connections, and the necessity of viewing his prophecies typologically: of seeing the past, things that "have been," as a type of the future, things that "will be." Used together, these keys enable us to penetrate the deepest mysteries of the book of Isaiah and in the process recognize the book for what it is, namely, a blueprint for the last days. I will first discuss the spirit and letter of prophecy.

The spirit of prophecy, which comes with the indwelling of the Holy Ghost (see 2 Peter 1:20, 21) and is synonymous with a testi-

mony that Jesus is the Christ (see Revelation 19:10), elucidates
and serves as a confirmation of the letter of prophecy. In the relevant passage from 2 Nephi 25:4, Nephi states, "The words of
Isaiah . . . are plain unto all those that are filled with the spirit of
prophecy." On the other hand, the letter of prophecy is a method
or "manner" of conveying the Lord's word and its interpretation
"taught" among the Jews, and must therefore be learned by us if
we want to understand. In 2 Nephi 25:5, Nephi states:

> I know that the Jews do understand the things of the prophets,
> and there is none other people that understand the things
> which were spoken unto the Jews like unto them, save it be that
> they are taught after the manner of the things of the Jews.

It is significant that the spirit and what I have called the letter of
prophecy are thus mentioned together, the spirit of prophecy being
a vertical approach to the scripture and the letter a horizontal
approach, each complementing the other.

Obtaining the spirit of prophecy, that is, obtaining personal
revelation through the Holy Ghost, is an essential feature of the
restored gospel of Jesus Christ, and is generally experienced beyond the application of the basic principles of the gospel. Its
dependence on the spiritual growth and worthiness of the person
receiving it renders its full treatment unnecessary here. Let it suffice to say that the Prophet Joseph Smith described the workings
of the Holy Ghost upon the mind as "strokes of pure intelligence
flowing into you,"[1] while Doctrine and Covenants 9:8 depicts the
action of the Holy Ghost as a burning of the bosom which serves to
confirm whether a thing is right and true. In the same light, Paul
maintains that the things of God are known only by the Spirit of
God (see 1 Corinthians 2:11), and that for mortals to comprehend
words written or uttered under the influence of the Holy Ghost,
they too must be touched by and possess that same Spirit (see 1
Corinthians 2:10-16). Although less dramatic in its operation, the
spirit of prophecy may be compared to the gift of tongues and to
that of the interpretation of tongues. Both are gifts of the same
Spirit (see 1 Corinthians 12:4-11), the prophet exercising the first
for our sake, and we the second if we would avail ourselves of it.

The letter of prophecy is essential to Jewish learning and includes a knowledge of "regions round about" the land of Israel

(see 2 Nephi 25:6). The concerted use of both the spirit and the letter of prophecy is prerequisite, however, to gaining a full understanding of the words of Isaiah, and thus several examples of the letter of prophecy will assist in clarifying this second key.

There exists today a fairly wide knowledge of the ancient Near East, the cradle or setting in which the prophecies of Isaiah were given. The literature we have from the ancient Near East is an indispensable resource for understanding Isaiah, not only because it yields a fuller account of ancient Near Eastern history than that contained in the Bible, but because it provides the clearest models of the literary forms and structures used in the composition of the book of Isaiah, as well as of the covenant theology which permeates it. Form criticism, which has preoccupied biblical scholars since the turn of the century, deals almost exclusively with identifying the various literary forms found in individual passages of the books of the prophets, prominently among them the book of Isaiah. Such forms, brought together by Claus Westermann,[2] include the Messenger Speech, the Lawsuit, the Proclamation of Judgment, the Woe Oracle, the Lament, the Ethical Sermon, and the Parable. Although the claims of liberal scholars on behalf of form criticism are excessive and often unsupported, we do learn from form-critical studies that virtually every passage in the book of Isaiah, down to its smallest components, is not part of a random accumulation of revelatory material, but instead possesses a recognizable literary form that is intended to convey a particular message.

This literary dimension alone would demand the highest respect for the book of Isaiah. It is, however, but one of several such literary dimensions, each of which is designed to convey a message or set of messages. In addition, the book contains a number of broad literary structures, each of which also conveys meaningful messages. Three of these broad structures are attested in literatures prevalent in parts of the ancient Near East before the time of Isaiah, and in the book of Isaiah all are superimposed upon one another, testifying to a carefully planned and highly sophisticated literary composition. A proper appreciation for this last literary dimension of the book of Isaiah prepares the way for viewing the book as an organic whole. Because all of these structures are based on various literary forms and plots, their total effect is a complex but clearly defined progression of thought comprehending the "end from the beginning" (see Isaiah 46:10) in which what is now ancient history in the book of Isaiah is subordinated editorially to a latter-day setting. In simple terms, this means that all that is prophesied in the book of Isaiah in its final edited state will be fulfilled in its entirety only in the latter days, and that it is in this latter-day context alone that we can legitimately and fully understand it. I will return to this concept in my discussion of the fourth key.

Central to Isaiah's thought is a theology of covenant, a theology also pertinent to the letter of prophecy, and consistent with ancient Near Eastern patterns prevalent in his day. At the root of biblical and Isaianic covenant theology lies the suzerain-vassal relationship defined in ancient Near Eastern political treaties, notably those of the Hittites and Assyrians. This relationship was first explored by Mendenhall in discussing the book of Deuteronomy and was seen elsewhere in the Old Testament by such scholars as Weinfeld, Calderone, and Fensham. The latter discovered that the covenant relationship between the Lord and his people Israel, and between the Lord and certain individuals, is similar to and appears to be modeled upon the ancient Near Eastern suzerain-vassal treaty (before 1400 B.C.). Within this relationship, the Lord, as suzerain or Great King, assured Israel, his vassal, of divine blessings, so long as Israel would abide by the terms of the covenant. Prominent among ancient Near Eastern covenant blessings was the suzerain's promise of an enduring inheritance of land by the vassal and his seed or offspring, and of protection in case of mortal danger. Israel, as the Lord's vassal, was called his "son" and "servant," reflecting, in part, the familial terms used in ancient Near Eastern treaties to define the suzerain-vassal relationship. Failure to abide by the terms of the covenant, on the other hand, paved the way for the prosecution of the vassal and the coming upon him of a long series of divine curses. The six-point literary formula of ancient Near Eastern treaties, including lists of blessings and curses (cf. Deuteronomy 28), was inscribed on tablets and duly sworn to by the parties concerned.[3]

As an illustration of this point, Job's companions were convinced of his transgression precisely because his calamities took the form of ancient Near Eastern covenant curses. However, Job proved to be an exception to the rule, and he thus served as a type of Christ. In Isaiah chapter 53 the suffering "servant" incurs the legal prosecution and covenant curses ensuing upon a vassal's failure to keep covenant, with the exception that there is mention in that chapter of his having "seed" or offspring (see Isaiah 53:10), signifying the innocence of the servant. Since the loss of seed or offspring was the first and major ancient Near Eastern covenant curse, such a loss would have meant that the servant was, in fact, guilty. But like Job, the Savior, whose atonement for transgression is herein prophesied, was an exception to the rule. Some idea of the larger influence of ancient Near Eastern covenant patterns in the book of Isaiah is indicated by the fact that virtually all the judgments of God enumerated in the book represent common ancient Near Eastern covenant curses.

A phenomenon in the book of Isaiah which does not appear in ancient Near Eastern treaty patterns, however, is that of curse reversals, such as barrenness turned to fertility (cf. Isaiah 5:6; 27:2, 3), famine to productivity (cf. Isaiah 3:1; 30:23), and darkness to light (cf. Isaiah 9:2; 60:1, 2). Curse reversals, brought about by divine intervention some time after the curses have been in effect, are an Isaianic phenomenon (as pointed out by Fensham) and constitute one of the book of Isaiah's most important identifying characteristics.

An entire vocabulary also forms part of the ancient Near Eastern background of Isaiah's covenant theology. Already noted is the "father-son" and "master-servant" relationship between the suzerain and the vassal. The verb "love," too, defines their relationship: if the vassal abides by the terms of the covenant, he is said to "love" the suzerain; if he does not, he is said to "rebel" against him. The suzerain, on his part, extends "mercy" and "compassion" to the vassal, both terms being ancient Near Eastern synonyms of covenant, as are "peace," "lovingkindness," "good," and "evil." The antithetical statement "I make peace and create evil" (Isaiah 45:7), therefore, need not cause any theological controversy over whether God created evil. "Peace," in ancient Near Eastern terminology, means covenant or covenant blessing, the Hebrew term "peace" *(salom)* possessing the additional meanings of "well-being" and "completeness." Within the same context, the Hebrew term "evil" *(ra ; ra a)* signifies covenant curse, and entirely lacks its English equivalent's connotation of an absolute, an abstract idea created in the minds of sophists and philosophers. So also, the exhortation to "do good" (see Isaiah 1:17), in the language of Isaiah, is an exhortation to keep covenant with the Lord, the rewards of such righteousness taking the form of covenant blessing, namely, eating the "good" of the land (Isaiah 1:19; cf. 3:10). Failure to "do good," on the other hand, brings "evil," or covenant curse, namely, the people's destruction (see Isaiah 1:20; cf. 3:9, 11), the Hebrew term "evil" (see above) possessing the additional meanings of "disaster," "calamity," and "misfortune." Throughout his book, Isaiah's theology presupposes this formal and enduring covenant relationship with the Lord, leaving no middle ground for those not for or against such a relationship.

As a work of prophetic poetry (except for a few biographical sections and one or two supplementary pieces of prose), the book of Isaiah is again better understood within its ancient Near Eastern background. The phenomenon of synonymous parallels, the chief feature of ancient Near Eastern poetry, assists in obtaining Isaiah's definition of a given term. In verses containing parallelisms, an idea or concept is generally stated twice, the second statement qualifying the first and vice versa. Within such parallelisms, each line commonly possesses a subject, a verb, and an object, each of which may function as a synonym of its parallel counterpart. Thus the expression "Zion shall be ransomed with justice and those of her who repent by righteousness" (Isaiah 1:27), by parallelism, defines "Zion" as "those of her who repent," a concept similarly stated in Isaiah 59:20. The phenomenon of antithetical parallels, on the other hand, as in the line "I make peace and create evil," assists in obtaining definitions of terms through contrast. What is important to this analytical approach is not necessarily what a term in Hebrew is purported to mean in the dictionary or lexicon, though that is important, but how Isaiah uses it in the text, what he intends to say by it, something I have called a "rhetorical definition." Essential to determining the meanings of terms based on this method, evidently, is some knowledge of Hebrew, or, alternately, the use of a translation consistently accurate against the Hebrew, if such exists. Having made my own translation of the Masoretic text of Isaiah into English, and in the process having compared every term employed in twelve of the most authoritative versions of the Bible, I retain strong reservations about depending for an interpretation on a single English translation of Isaiah, as one translation alone can never say all that the Hebrew says.

Although "Zion," as we saw above, is identified indirectly by parallelism as those of Israel who repent and are ransomed (see Isaiah 1:27), it is elsewhere identified directly as the place of return for the ransomed of the Lord (see Isaiah 35:10; 51:11). A total Isaianic definition of Zion thus consists of both a people and a place—both narrowly defined within Isaiah's scheme of a latter-day deliverance. Juxtaposed with Zion is "Babylon," a term defined by context. Chapter 13 of Isaiah, purportedly about Babylon (cf. Isaiah 13:1), nevertheless identifies its subject as "sinners," "the world," "the wicked," and so forth (see Isaiah 13:9, 11), while in the same chapter a divine judgment upon Babylon implies a judgment upon the entire earth (see Isaiah 13:13, 14). Thus, like Zion, the term "Babylon" represents both a people and a place, though the latter is evidently much more broadly defined. The juxtaposition of Zion and Babylon in the book of Isaiah, a juxtaposition which takes various forms,[4] allows us to obtain a further definition of each by virtue of their contrast. According to this contrast, Zion is by inference what Babylon is not, and Babylon, by the same token, is what Zion is not. If Babylon in the book of Isaiah consists of the wicked of the world who are destroyed in a day of universal judgment (see Isaiah 13:9, 11, 13, 14), then Zion must be the righteous of the earth who are saved in this universal judgment. On the other hand, if Zion consists of those of the Lord's people who repent, are ransomed, and return home (see Isaiah 1:27; 35:10), then Babylon must be those who do not repent, nor are ransomed, nor return home.

Isaiah's extensive use of metaphors forms an integral part of the letter of prophecy. In the verse, "Hark! a tumult on the mountains, as of a vast multitude. Hark! an uproar among kingdoms, as of nations assembling" (Isaiah 13:4), the parallel occurrence of the terms "mountains" and "kingdoms" denotes "mountains" to be a metaphor of "kingdoms," a concept similarly stated in Isaiah 64:1-3, where the term "mountains" appears as a metaphor of "nations." This concept has important implications in a passage such as Isaiah 2:14, where the cataclysm of nature, in the form of the levelling of high mountains in the day of the Lord's coming in power, carries with it as well the idea of social upheaval. In this passage, the levelling of high mountains allegorically implies a levelling of exalted kingdoms or nations. Interestingly, the Book of Mormon version of the passage actually includes this idea within a series of geophysical objects (cf. 2 Nephi 12:14cd).

The same allegorical identity of mountains as nations allows one to read the idea of world political prominence into the passage in Isaiah 2:2 dealing with the "mountain" in which the law and word of the Lord are restored. According to the Hebrew, the passage reads: "In the latter days the mountain of the Lord's house shall become established as/in the head/top of the mountains," the Hebrew term *ro s* having as its primary meaning the English word "head," and as secondary meanings the words "chief" and "top." The Hebrew preposition *be,* translated "in" in the King James Version, is considered a *bet essentiae* by most scholars, and could thus be translated "as." Not surprisingly, it actually occurs as the preposition *ke,* meaning "as," in the Dead Sea scroll of Isaiah, IQIsa[a]. In the Sinai covenant, Israel was promised as a covenant blessing that it would become the "head" of the nations (cf. Deuteronomy 28:10, 13). We see, therefore, that two valid but different interpretations are possible from a single passage in Isaiah, both of which contribute to an understanding of events in the latter days. On the one hand, we find the idea of world political prominence centered in the nation in which the law and word of the Lord are restored, while on the other we find the actual spiritual center of that restoration located in the tops of the mountains, a geographical location.

Isaiah's use of metaphors extends to a group of royal metaphors designating the king of Assyria/Babylon and the Davidic king.[5] Both appear under the guise of the "hand" of the Lord—the (left) "hand" of punishment (cf. Isaiah 5:25; 10:4; 14:26), or the royal executioner of ancient Near Eastern tradition, and the (right) "hand" of deliverance (cf. Isaiah 11:11, 15; 41:10, 13), or the royal executive (cf. Psalm 80:17). Both appear as a royal "ensign" or "banner" (Heb. *nes*), the one rallying wicked nations from beyond the horizon to punish the Lord's people for their wickedness (see Isaiah 5:26; 13:2), the other rallying the righteous from among all nations to Zion (see Isaiah 11:10, 12; 49:22), a safe place in the day of judgment. The king of Assyria/Babylon also appears as the "rod" and "staff" of the Lord's punishment (see Isaiah 10:5; 14:5), and the Davidic king as a staff and "flagellum" to punish this tyrant (see Isaiah 10:26). All of these terms are royal metaphors. The king of Assyria/Babylon again appears under the metaphors of the Lord's "anger" and "wrath," of which he is the instrument (cf. Isaiah 5:25; 10:5; 13:5, 9), and as an "ax" and "saw" to hew down the wicked (see Isaiah 10:15; 14:8; 37:24). The Davidic king consistently appears as the Lord's "righteousness" (cf. Isaiah 41:2, 10; 51:5), a divine and royal attribute and forerunner of "salvation" (see Isaiah 46:13; 56:1); the latter is a metaphor for the Lord himself (see Isaiah 12:2; 62:11). The king of Assyria and his confederation of wicked nations are further depicted as "River" (*Nahar;* see Isaiah 8:7; 11:15) and "Sea" (*Yamm;* see Isaiah 5:30; 10:26; 17:12), well-known powers of Chaos of ancient Near Eastern mythology. In the same context, also mythological, the Davidic king is portrayed as a "light" illuminating the darkness of those in captivity (see Isaiah 9:2; 42:6; 49:6), representing a power of Creation. Distinct patterns of alternating themes of Chaos and Creation in the book of Isaiah tell of the Davidic king's eventual victory over the forces of Chaos.[6]

The letter of prophecy, then, assists in unravelling what several ancient sources call the "hidden things" spoken by Isaiah (Sir. Isaiah 48:25), a message "recorded in parables" to hide its intent from the worldly wise (Asc. Isaiah 4:20). The prophecy that Israel, when strengthened by the "right hand" of the Lord (Isaiah 41:10, 13), will thresh "mountains" into "dust" and into "chaff" (Isaiah 41:15) need present no difficulty when the various terms used are recognized for what they are. The terms "dust" and "chaff" are chaos motifs, signifying that Israel and its Davidic king (cf. Isaiah 41:2, 25), the "right hand" of the Lord (Isaiah 41:10, 13), will make chaos of the wicked nations when they have served the Lord's purpose in punishing Israel. It is important to keep in mind with regard to the letter of prophecy that the book of Isaiah contains built-in checks in the form of parallelisms and other interrelationships that assist the reader in avoiding the pitfalls of spurious interpretation. The letter of prophecy is both inductive and verifiable; it is a principle of interpretation which builds upon itself, but which is always in harmony with other scriptural principles of interpretation. Where the letter of prophecy is applied consistently, and where its use is inspired and influenced by the spirit of prophecy, a vast wealth of information pertinent to and essential for the last days unfolds to the reader from the words of Isaiah.

This leads to a third key opening up a new dimension for understanding Isaiah, namely, the Savior's commandment to diligently search his words. After quoting Isaiah at length, the Savior states: "I say unto you that ye ought to search these things. Yea, a commandment I give unto you that ye search these things diligently; for great are the words of Isaiah." (3 Nephi 23:1.) The command to search diligently the words of Isaiah is plainly intended to mean something other than an emphasis upon the necessity of reading them. It implies that without a concerted inquiry one cannot properly understand the words of Isaiah, and ultimately that nothing less than an all-out investigation will yield the desired results. It means that Isaiah's words are too "great" to be comprehended by a surface reading only. His book exhibits all the characteristics of a great literary masterpiece and, as such, requires serious effort to be understood. The Savior's recommendation assures us that the knowledge to be gained is worth the effort.

As has just been briefly demonstrated, the letter of prophecy necessarily involves a diligent searching of the scripture, for without it we cannot apply the letter of prophecy. We have seen that it is impossible to determine Isaiah's use of words as metaphors, or to arrive at a rhetorical definition of terms, without searching the text. Similarly, we have seen that one cannot understand some of the deeper implications of the book of Isaiah without a working knowledge of its ancient Near Eastern context and of the author's view of this context as an underlying presupposition, and, in that light, conducting a search of the text for informative underlying parallels. Again, we have been made aware that it is impossible to discern the various literary forms and structures employed in the book of Isaiah, and the message conveyed by each, except by a diligent search based on a knowledge of similar forms and structures in other literatures. Finally, it is evident to one who has studied a Hebrew biblical text that one cannot gain a full idea of the language of Isaiah from a translation alone. To better understand it, one must come to terms with the Hebrew and so capture the various levels and nuances of meaning conveyed by the prophet's choice of words. This, again, requires diligent searching.

The last point can be readily demonstrated in each and every verse of the Book of Isaiah; but for the sake of brevity, I will cite only a few examples from the sixth chapter of Isaiah. In it, there is a description of "seraphs" about the throne of the Lord (Heb. *seraphim;* see Isaiah 6:2), a term meaning "fiery ones" or serpents (Heb. *serapim;* cf. Numbers 21:6, 8; Deuteronomy 8:15; Isaiah 14:29). The latter are evidently intended to serve as a symbol for the kind of seraphs spoken of in Isaiah chapter 6; their peculiar name perhaps characterizes them, in the language of the Prophet Joseph Smith, as beings who "dwell amid everlasting burnings."[7] These "fiery ones" are depicted as having "wings" (Heb. *kenapayim*), a biblical term which also means "veils" or "covers." Indeed, with these "wings" they can "veil," "cover," or "hide" (Heb. *yekasseh*) their "face" (Heb. *panaw*), a term which also means "presence." Further, they can hide their "feet" or "legs" (Heb. *raglaw*), which may equally refer to their "footing," the place where they are standing, or simply their "location." Lastly, they have the power to "fly about" (Heb. *ye opep*), but this is not necessarily a reference to flying like birds by means of flapping wings! What we have here, in reality, is not a description of some bizarre creatures unknown to us, but of angels and their power to conceal themselves from men and to move freely through space. In the manner of angels, they sing a hymn of praise, beginning with "Holy, holy, holy is the Lord of hosts" (Isaiah 6:3). The threefold occurrence of the adjective "holy" represents the superlative, which has no other means of expression in biblical Hebrew. A more correct translation would therefore be "Most holy is the Lord of hosts," including all the overtones of meaning of the various terms used.

The next line of the verse, "the whole earth is full of his glory," is probably an inadequate translation of the text (Heb. *melo kol ha ares kebodo*) based on what various translators thought it signified. Such mistranslations are often the case when translators are at a loss as to the sense or doctrine of a particular phrase. A knowledge of the restored gospel of Jesus Christ often assists in arriving at a more correct translation. In the present example, the world translated "full" (Heb. *melo*) is not an adjective, but is the noun "fulfillment," and its synonyms are "fulness" and "consummation." In the biblical text, moreover, this noun, not the noun "earth," is the subject of the sentence. A literal translation of the passage, therefore, is "the consummation of the whole earth is his glory," or even, "the fulfillment of the full measure of the earth is his glory." These renderings are more in harmony with the restored gospel's teachings concerning the earth fulfilling the measure of its creation, and concerning this purpose of the creation as the Lord's work and glory.

One could go on at length expounding the problems and mechanics of translation and their usually negative effect on the meaning conveyed to the reader, but two more examples must suffice. Verse 5 of chapter 6 mentions Isaiah's being struck "dumb" (Heb. *nidmeti*), an expression commonly translated "undone" or "ruined." Actually two Hebrew roots are possible, *nadam* and *dama,* the first meaning "silenced" or "made dumb," the second meaning "perished" or "ruined." The fact that the prophet "said" what he did (Heb. *omar*) may simply mean that he "thought" it to himself; both definitions are valid renderings of the Hebrew verb. The idea of Isaiah's being struck dumb makes more sense than his perishing, not only because he actually survives, but in light of the opening-of-the-mouth rite which follows (see Isaiah 6:6, 7), preparatory to his commission as a prophet (see Isaiah 6:8, 9). A rite of the "opening of the mouth" is also found in ancient Near Eastern texts as an Egyptian temple ritual.[8]

A final example of problems in translation of the Hebrew is from verse 13 of chapter 6. There a "tenth" of the people are depicted as remaining in the land or returning to their cities and homes after a great calamity has taken place (cf. Isaiah 6:11, 12). But this tenth itself is "burned"; the Hebrew term (*leba er*) has three distinct meanings, two of which apply directly. The King James Version's rendering of it as "eaten" is doubtless based on the verb's secondary meaning of "annihilated" or "consumed"; its primary meaning is "burned," as has been mentioned. In this verse, some of the people are represented as surviving this "burning" or "annihilation" of the tenth, the tenth itself being likened to a "terebinth" tree (Heb. *ela*) or an "oak" (Heb. *alon*), whose "stump" (Heb. *massebet*) remains alive when the tree is "cut down" or "felled" (Heb. *salleket*). The King James Version's rendering of the word "stump" (Heb. *massebet*) as "substance" is again based on a secondary meaning in the Hebrew, its primary meaning being "that which stands erect," such as a "pillar" or a "stump"; in its present context it refers to that which is left standing. In other words, the "holy seed," left standing after a twofold calamity, is likened to the stump of a terebinth or an oak, each having the capacity to grow into new trees after it is cut down. This "holy seed" or "consecrated offspring" (Heb. *zera quodes*) is to become a new tree, symbolizing a new Israel, if we pardon the prophet's habitual mixing of metaphors! The key word in this verse is the "tenth" (Heb. *asiriya*), a term which also means "tithe" (Heb. *asiri*). As any learned Jew can tell you, the unusual *ya* ending further signifies that it is a special tithe, the "tithe of *ya*," or Jehovah. In other words, Isaiah is using the imagery of the tithe of the tithe. Anciently, the Israelites paid a tithe of their increase to the Levites, who, in turn, paid a tithe to the priests, the family of Aaron (see Numbers 18:24-29). The "holy seed" in verse 13 thus represents the tithe of the tithe, anciently called the "holy portion," the portion consecrated to Jehovah (see Numbers 18:26). It is this 1 percent of the population that wholly escapes destruction on the Lord's day of judgment.

The commandment to search the words of Isaiah also extends to applying an acute discernment to what is being said between the lines. An example of this in chapter 6 is the significance of the cleansing ember taken with tongs from the altar (see verse 6). The altar is that of atonement, and Isaiah's remission of sins (verse 7) is thus by virtue of that atonement. Furthermore, the location of this scene of atonement between two verses in which Isaiah both sees and hears the Lord (verses 5 and 8) must be considered significant to this atonement. Verse 10 contains the Lord's prediction of the general reaction of the people to Isaiah's prophesying, in which Isaiah is in the unfortunate role of hardener of the heart. But it also contains a five-point formula for salvation, namely, seeing with the eyes, hearing with the ears, understanding with the "mind" or "heart" (Heb. *lebab*), "returning" or "repenting" (Heb. *sab*), and being healed. This leaves the door open for the deliverance of at least a righteous remnant, namely, those who follow this formula. This indeed proves to be the case (cf. Isaiah 10:21, 22).

An interesting example of what may be found by reading between the lines occurs in verses 11 and 12 of Isaiah chapter 1. At the beginning of verse 11 the "purpose" or the "why" (Heb. *lamma*) of temple-going is asked. The answer is provided at the beginning of verse 12 in the line, "When you come to see me." The active verb (Heb. *lir ot*) has been given a passive vocalization by the Masoretes (Heb. *lera ot*; viz., "to appear") in contradistinction to the proper passive form of the verb (Heb. *lehera ot*), suggesting that the Masoretes did not believe that the people could actually *see* the Lord in the temple. The verb "to see" is followed in the text by the direct object "my face" (Heb. *panai*), which also means "my presence," or simply "me." This confirms that the active form of the verb "to see" is the correct one, as no intervening preposition appears in the Hebrew text. The "purpose" of temple-going, therefore, according to Isaiah, is to be received into the "presence" of the Lord.

Another and final dimension of searching the words of Isaiah consists of the recognition of key words. The passage predicting the restoration of the gospel in the latter days cited earlier, for example (see Isaiah 2:2-5), contains in each of its four verses a key word linking this passage to Israel's return from dispersion. In verse 2, the verb "flow" or "stream" (Heb. *naharu*) characterizes "nations" or "Gentiles" (Heb. *goyim*) streaming to Zion. But why did Isaiah choose this particular verb in favor of more common verbs, such as "go" and "come"? He did so because both the word "flow" and the key idea of nations or Gentiles streaming to Zion occur in other, related contexts in the book of Isaiah. In Isaiah 60:5 and 66:12, they appear in the context of Israel's return, but without any time identification such as "the latter days" in Isaiah 2:2. This textual correlation involving the term "flow" accomplishes two things. First, it identifies the streaming of the nations to Zion in Isaiah 2:2 with Israel's return, an idea not explicitly stated in that verse; and secondly, it identifies the return in Isaiah 60:5

and 66:12 with the latter days, an idea not stated there. This does away with the necessity seen by scholars, for example, of linking Israel's return to the Jews' historical return from Babylon and the resultant linking of the greater part of Isaiah's prophecies with the remote past. It also reemphasizes the fact that Isaiah did not always write in plain terms, and demonstrates particularly well the necessity of searching the text for clues to better understanding.

Verse 3 of Isaiah chapter 2 again links the scene of representatives of all nations going to Zion to the idea of Israel's return. The verb "go up" or "ascend" in this verse (Heb. *na aleh*) is a pilgrimage motif and key word. Two or three times a year, in the seasons of religious festivals, the ancient Israelites "went up" or "ascended" to Jerusalem from throughout the land of Israel to make a pilgrimage to the temple of the Lord (see Psalm 122:1-4; cf. Zechariah 14:16-18). This pilgrimage was traditionally made in remembrance of the exodus out of Egypt under Moses, the period of wandering in the wilderness, and the return to the land of the fathers under Joshua. Later, it became a prophetic type of the latter-day return of Israel from throughout the earth (cf. Jeremiah 31:6), and Isaiah uses the imagery of a pilgrimage to Zion in this very context in 30:29; 35:8-10; and 51:10, 11. By means of the key verb "go up" or "ascend" in Isaiah 2:3, he thus again identifies the idea of Israel's return with the scene of the nations going to Zion depicted in this verse, and the return itself with a latter-day setting.

Similarly, the verb "judge" or "arbitrate" (Heb. *sapat*) in verse 4 occurs elsewhere in the book of Isaiah, but only in contexts in which Israel's return has already taken place and its king rules (cf. Isaiah 11:3, 4; 16:5; 51:5). In verse 5, the term "light" (Heb. *or*) is a key word linking this verse to a scene of Israel's return from throughout the earth in Isaiah 60:1-4. There the "light" is the glory of the Lord which attracts "nations" and "rulers," "sons" and "daughters" to Zion. In another context in the book of Isaiah, the "light" is the law itself, going forth as divine "precepts" to all nations (51:4), and in yet another, mentioned previously, it is a metaphor for the Davidic king. Every one of these definitions of the term "light" can and must be applied to Isaiah 2:5 in order for the verse to be fully understood. Needless to say, this is not possible without diligent searching or, for that matter, without the spirit and the letter of prophecy, a principle of interpretation that over-laps all others.

A fourth key, given in conjunction with the key of searching, is that Isaiah spoke of things that "have been and shall be." In 3 Nephi 23:3 the Savior stated, "All things that he [Isaiah] spake have been and shall be, even according to the words which he spake." One interpretation of this statement is that doubtless some of Isaiah's prophecies were fulfilled in his own day, while others remained to be fulfilled. But the Savior's peculiar description of all things spoken by Isaiah as things that "have been and shall be" occurs elsewhere in the scriptures only to denote a typological view of history. The writer of Ecclesiastes expounded the idea that what has been is a type of what shall be. I quote from Ecclesiastes 1:9: "That which has been shall be; that which was done shall be done: there is nothing at all that is new under the sun." This accords with the traditional Jewish method or "manner" of interpreting the written prophecies, namely, that of seeing them as applicable on at least two time planes: first, the historical situation prevailing in the prophet's own day, to which his prophecies formulate a response; and second, the latter days, of which the ancient events of Israelite history are a type.[9]

So Nephi, who understood that many prophecies of Isaiah, up to and including the Babylonian captivity, had already been ful-filled in his day (cf. 2 Nephi 25:10), spoke as if the prophecies of Isaiah had yet to see fulfillment. After quoting Isaiah at length, he made the statement that "in the days that the prophecies of Isaiah shall be fulfilled men shall know of a surety" (2 Nephi 25:7); in conjunction with this he claimed that "they shall be of great worth unto them in the last days; for in that day shall they understand them; wherefore, for their good have I written them" (2 Nephi 25:8). The prophecies which Nephi had just written, however, were chapters 2 to 14 of Isaiah, prophecies which, for the most part, related to the period before the Babylonian captivity. There thus appears to be a contradiction in his words, unless it is realized that Nephi, too, as a Jew, viewed the words of Isaiah typologically. Perhaps the strongest evidence for this typological view of the prophecies of Isaiah consists of the various superimposed literary structures to which I referred previously. The existence of these structures, which span the length of the book, not only attests to a master plan of composition, a broad literary framework to which an original collection of prophecies has been subordinated, but establishes an entirely new plane for their interpretation, one that transcends their historical relevance and allows us to re-read them in an eschatological or latter-day context.

From the Savior's statement that Isaiah spoke of things which "have been and shall be," we infer that the ancient events of biblical history were a type of those to come. Isaiah himself uses the major events of biblical history as themes upon which to build his prophecies. Just as there was anciently a Chaos, a Creation, a Flood, and a Destruction of Sodom and Gomorrah, so, according to Isaiah, there will be a New Chaos, a New Creation, a New Flood, and a New Sodom and Gomorrah Destruction, though in a different order. Just as there was anciently a Passover, an Exodus, a Descensus of the Lord on the Mount, and a Wandering in the Wilderness, so there will be a New Passover, a New Exodus, a New Descensus, a New Wandering in the Wilderness, and, in effect, a new version of every other event that constituted a historical precedent. The Lord asked through Isaiah, "Who foretells what happens as I do, and is the equal of me in appointing a people from of old as types, foreshadowing things to come?" (Isaiah 44:7.) It is this coming together of all the ancient types, in fact, that characterizes the last days, enabling those who live through that time to apply the prophecies of Isaiah to their own situations for their profit and learning more than any previous generation.

On the basis of the key that "what has been shall be," one may therefore conclude that, with regard to prophecies concerning the events of his own day, Isaiah spoke on two levels, the first pertaining to what was then transpiring, the second to the latter days. Both periods of Israel's history were seen by the prophet in vision (cf. Sir. Isaiah 48:25), and thus he prophesied of "all things" concerning the Lord's people, according to the Savior (3 Nephi 23:2). Isaiah's literary genius, or that which made his words "great" (3 Nephi 23:1), was his inspired competence at including both his own time and the last days in a single prophecy, one in which the former events served as the type of the latter.

   This key of interpreting the prophecies of the book of Isaiah typologically is necessary in order to understand the modern relevance of ancient names and entities such as Assyria, characterized by Isaiah as the great world power from the north, the first to conquer the world (except Zion/Jerusalem) by military force; Egypt, the greatest political and military power up to that time, to whose vast force of horsemen and chariots other nations look for protection in the day of the Assyrian flood; Babylon, characterized as a great materialistic and idolatrous world dominion, representing all that is destroyed in a fiery holocaust; Zion, a new Israel created out of the chaos of Babylon, comprising the righteous who participate in a New Exodus out of Babylon before destruction comes. By means of this great key to the book of Isaiah, we may read the names of ancient entities as code names for latter-day entities, providing an invaluable source of knowledge for those who will see the events so foreshadowed.

   It is my belief that by extending our search to decoding and correlating the contents of the book of Isaiah, we are able to unseal the message of this enigmatic book. It is also my belief that although the above keys for understanding Isaiah are scholarly in nature, their application is by no means limited to scholars. We may each apply them for our own benefit, gaining insights perhaps completely overlooked by so-called experts in the field. While some of the views I have expressed may eventually be modified, I am convinced that to the degree of our obedience to the Lord's commandments as we apply the above keys, and to the degree that we possess the Holy Spirit, which comes of this obedience, no scripture in the book of Isaiah will remain hidden from our eyes, and every interpretation may be put to the test.

Notes

   1. *Teachings of the Prophet Joseph Smith,* sel. Joseph Fielding Smith (Salt Lake City: Deseret Book Company, 1938), p. 151.

   2. Claus Westermann, *Basic Forms of Prophetic Speech* (1966).

   3. *Theological Dictionary of the Old Testament* (1975), 2:266-69.

   4. Avraham Gileadi, "A Holistic Structure of the Book of Isaiah" (Ph.D. dissertation, Brigham Young University, 1981).

5. Avraham Gileadi, *The Apocalyptic Book of Isaiah: A New Translation with Interpretative Key* (Provo, Utah: Hebraeus Press, 1982).

6. For a fuller study of this idea see Gileadi, "A Holistic Structure of the Book of Isaiah."

7. *Teachings of the Prophet Joseph Smith*, p. 347.

8. See Hugh Nibley, *The Message of the Joseph Smith Papyri: An Egyptian Endowment* (Salt Lake City: Deseret Book Company, 1975).

9. See Daniel Patte, *Early Jewish Hermeneutic in Palestine* (Missoula, Mont.: Scholars Press, 1975).

8

The Prophets and the Mission

Ellis T. Rasmussen

There is nothing unusual about peoples or cultures considering themselves chosen of the gods, having some special privileged relationship with a special deity, with some designated responsibility imposed through a covenant with him. It has been quite common throughout the ages. It may have had its origin in the relationships of our first ancestors with the Creator. As we see from the record of human and divine relationships portrayed in our Judeo-Christian scriptures, not only Adam but his patriarchal successors enjoyed a covenantal relationship with the Lord. Through it they knew what they could expect from him and what their duty to him was, to perpetuate his good way of life. They expected this relationship to bring benefits in this world and membership in his eternal kingdom to come. (See Moses 5:6-12, 14-15; 6:22-23.) Many peoples since then have assumed such relationships, and some have been quite bigoted in their religious self-view. Those who have not had the true concept of the universal Father who cares for all people have thought they were chosen and would be blessed because of who they were. Some invented local gods concerned only with local people. Sometimes even the true heirs of the patriarchs developed false ideas about their status and mission. The chosen people of the living God were really chosen to bring salvation to all other people, other families, other nations.

This concept is nowhere better expressed than in the scriptural records of Abraham's call:

Now the Lord had said unto Abram,
Get thee out of thy country
and from thy kindred,
and from thy father's house,
unto a land that I will shew thee:
And I will make of thee a great nation,
and I will bless thee and make thy name great;
and thou shalt be a blessing:
And I will bless them that bless thee
and curse him that curseth thee:
and *in thee shall all families of the earth be blessed.*
> (Genesis 12:1-3; italics in this and succeeding
> scriptural quotations added for emphasis.)

The matter is made even more explicit in another passage, this one from Abraham's own record:

Behold, I will lead thee by my hand,
and I will take thee,
to put upon thee my name,
even the Priesthood of thy father,
and my power shall be over thee.
As it was with Noah so shall it be with thee;
but through thy ministry
my name shall be known in the earth forever,
for I am thy God.
> (Abraham 1:18-19.)

And I will make of thee a great nation,
and I will bless thee above measure,
and make thy name great *among all nations,*
and thou shalt be a blessing unto thy seed after thee,
that in their hands *they shall bear this ministry and
   Priesthood*
unto all nations.
And I will bless them through thy name;
for as many as receive this Gospel
shall be called after thy name,
and shall be accounted thy seed,
and shall rise up and bless thee, as their father;
And I will bless them that bless thee,
and curse them that curse thee;
and in thee (that is, in thy Priesthood)
and in thy seed (that is, thy Priesthood),

for I give unto thee a promise
that this right shall continue in thee,
and in thy seed after thee (that is to say, the literal seed, or
   the seed of the body)
shall all the families of the earth be blessed,
even with the blessings of the Gospel,
which are the blessings of salvation,
even of life eternal.

(Abraham 2:9-11.)

Moses and the prophets of Israel reiterated, perpetuated, defined, and clarified this concept—that to be chosen of God is to be
appointed to his service. According to them, as we may see in the
scriptures, the chosen in any age of the world may expect blessings
and divine favor only as rewards for service. The contract or covenant of the chosen with God may be simply stated: If you will be
my messengers and exemplars, I will be your teacher, guide, and
defender, and I will prosper you.

Moses revealed these things quite precisely to Israel's hosts
encamped at Sinai when he was trying to get them ready to assume
their functions as God's servants. In the words of God, he said:

Ye have seen what I did unto the Egyptians,
and how I bare you on eagles' wings,
and brought you unto myself.
Now therefore,
if ye will obey my voice indeed,
and keep my covenant,
then ye shall be a *peculiar treasure* unto me above all people:
for all the earth is mine:
And ye shall be unto me *a kingdom of priests,* and *an holy*
   nation.

(Exodus 19:4-6.)

Later, in his farewell address before his departure from his
people at Mount Nebo, Moses charged them to be obedient:

Behold, I have taught you statutes and judgments,
even as the Lord my God commanded me,
that ye should do so in the land whither ye go to possess it.
Keep therefore and do them;
for this is your wisdom and your understanding
in the sight of the nations,
which shall hear all these statutes, and say,
Surely this great nation

is a wise and understanding people.
For what nation is there so great,
who hath God so nigh unto them,
as the Lord our God is
in all things that we call upon him for?
And what nation is there so great,
that hath statutes and judgments
so righteous as all this law,
which I set before you this day?

(Deuteronomy 4:5-8.)

Lest the Lord's calling and appointment of the Israelites to serve
him should cause them to feel proud and become bigoted, Moses
also warned them in the words of the Lord:

Not for thy righteousness,
or for the uprightness of thine heart,
dost thou go to possess their land:
but for the wickedness of these nations
the Lord thy God doth drive them out from before thee
and that he may perform the word
which the Lord sware unto thy fathers, Abraham, Isaac, and
    Jacob.

(Deuteronomy 9:5.)

Moses indeed continually lectured the Israelites on this matter,
citing historical examples of their transgressions and other inade-
quacies, and calling on them to repent and teach the law by their
works as well as their words.

The chosen people were to teach others the good law and true
worship, but were not to let those others teach them unrighteous
ways and idolatrous worship. Moses usually gave the Israelites
that admonition when he warned them not to marry the daughters
or sons of other peoples. He warned that such marriage partners
would too easily turn them away from their responsibilities to the
true God and turn them to the easier, lustful, sensually exciting
ways of the fertility gods and goddesses. (For examples, see
Exodus 34:14-16 and Deuteronomy 7:3-6. Many more examples
may be found in the Topical Guide to the scriptures, published in
the appendix of the LDS edition of the Bible, under such topics as
"Idolatry" and "Israel, Mission of.")

It was some seven centuries after Moses that the great writing
prophets wrote the books known as the major and minor prophetic

works of the Old Testament, most of which came in two waves in the eighth and seventh centuries B.C. Those were the grim days of apostasy when Israel's northern tribes and their kings, and later the remaining Israelite nation of Judah, turned aside to idolatrous theologies and morals. The prophets were called to preach repentance and to call the chosen people to return to their covenant mission. Their prophetic messages were written to the Israelites of their own time, but they are valid for any era; indeed, they address many teachings, promises, and warnings to descendants and heirs of the Abrahamic mission in the last days.

In this matter, as in many others, Isaiah pronounced the message most clearly. In a great arraignment of Israel, preserved as the first chapter of the book of Isaiah, he charged the Israelites with rebellion against God; they were "laden with iniquity"; their children were "corrupters"; they had "gone away backward," learning and doing the abominations of the wicked instead of converting the wicked to the Lord's good way of life (see Isaiah 1:2-4). Their leaders were as the "rulers of Sodom," and the people following them were as the "people of Gomorrah"; therefore their sacrifices were "vain oblations"; their sabbaths, assemblies, feasts, and even their prayers were seen as hypocritical and unacceptable to God (see Isaiah 1:13-15). Yet even then, if they would wash (the familiar ritual of an outer washing symbolic of an inner cleansing), "cease to do evil," and "learn to do well," by doing good to and for others, then the Lord would be willing to "reason together" with them. Through repentance the miracle of forgiveness was still available, even though their "sins be as scarlet" and "red like crimson." They could still be blessed to "eat the good of the land." But if they refused to repent and rebelled further, they would "be devoured with the sword." And this message was not merely Isaiah's opinion, for, as he concluded, "the mouth of the Lord hath spoken it." (See Isaiah 1:16-20.)

A little earlier, during the reigns of King Uzziah of Judah and King Jeroboam of Israel, Amos similarly gave all Israel, north and south, a scathing prophetic rebuke and a call to repentance. The Lord had called him from following the flocks near Tekoa and from harvesting the sycamore fig (the tree has a mulberry-like leaf and a small fig-like fruit which must be scored or pierced to ripen and sweeten) in the lower valleys of Judah. His charge was, "Go, prophesy unto my people Israel'' (Amos 7:15). Amos's response was direct; he cried to the recreant priests and people, ''Now therefore hear thou the word of the Lord'' (Amos 7:16). He set both his native tribe of Judah and her ten sister tribes to the north into the same evil context as six of their decadent neighbors, making the Israelite nations numbers seven and eight on his list— symbolizing a full roster plus one. He blamed them as he blamed each of the neighboring gentile nations ''for three transgressions . . . and for four.'' Three symbolized fulness, and four symbolized overflowing evil in each of the seven nations plus one! (See Amos 1:3-2:8.)

As Ezekiel later observed, the chosen people had become like the other nations of Canaan—as if the Amorites had fathered them and the Hittites had mothered them (see Ezekiel 16:3, 45). They had beome children of their environment and had forgotten what it meant to be a child of God.

Amos said that the people of Judah had ''despised the law of the Lord''; they had ''not kept his commandments''; their ''lies caused them to err'' (Amos 2:4). Northern Israel he charged with selling righteous and poor people; cheating poor and meek people; committing immorality, infidelity, and idolatry; and profaning the holy name of the Lord (see Amos 2:4-8). With irony he declaimed, ''You only have I known of all the families of the earth: therefore I will punish you for all your iniquities'' (Amos 3:2). They had known their God and his law, and they had known his blessings; therefore more had been expected of them.

Hosea, who also prophesied in the reigns of Uzziah, Jotham, Ahaz, and Hezekiah of Judah and the last six kings of Israel, summed up the evils of the apostate chosen people with chilling succinctness:

> Hear the word of the Lord, ye children of Israel: for the Lord hath a controversy with the inhabitants of the land, because there is no truth, nor mercy, nor knowledge of God in the Land.
>
> By swearing, and lying, and killing, and stealing, and committing adultery, they break out, and blood toucheth blood.
>
> Therefore shall the land mourn, and every one that dwelleth therein shall languish, with the beasts of the field, and with the fowls of heaven; yea, the fishes of the sea also shall be taken away. (Hosea 4:1-3.)

For such failing in their calling, such perversions, and such abominations, the northern tribes of Israel would be lost until the last days of the world. Only then would remnants of their descendants be gathered together "and appoint themselves one head"; then at last would it "come to pass, that in the place where it was said unto them, Ye are not my people, there it shall be said unto them, Ye are the sons of the living God" (see Hosea 1:6-7, 9-11). But in the interim, as Ezekiel later observed, they would be "scattered through the countries" and remain "among the nations whither they shall be carried captives" until, as the Lord said, "you shall remember me" (Ezekiel 6:8-9).

Now, what is it that Israel should have done as a chosen people, and what part of the mission remains for the latter-day covenant people of the Lord to do?

Both Isaiah and his young contemporary, Micah, gave us a picture of the situation in the last days when at last the mission will begin to be fulfilled:

And it shall come to pass in the last days,
that the mountain of the Lord's house
shall be established in the top of the mountains,
and shall be exalted above the hills;
and *all nations* shall flow unto it.
And *many people* shall go and say,
Come ye, and let us go up to the mountain of the Lord,
to the house of the God of Jacob;
and he will teach us of his ways,
and we will walk in his paths:
for out of Zion shall go forth the law,
and the word of the Lord from Jerusalem.
And he shall *judge among the nations,*
and shall *rebuke many people:*
and they shall beat their swords into plowshares,
and their spears into pruninghooks:
nation shall not lift up sword against nation,
neither shall they learn war any more.
O house of Jacob, come ye,
and let us walk in the light of the Lord.
(Isaiah 2:2-5; compare Micah 4:1-7.)

The concept that all nations, all families of the earth, will enjoy the blessings of affiliation in covenant relationships with the God whom Israel served, and with the Davidic Messiah to come, is also seen in Isaiah's picture of that peaceful time told in the words of chapter 11 of his book: the "root of Jesse" will indeed provide an ensign for all peoples; he will "set up an ensign for *the nations,* and shall assemble the outcasts of *Israel,* and gather together the dispersed of *Judah* from the four corners of the earth" (Isaiah 11:10, 12). In a later passage Isaiah dramatically depicted the peaceable assimilation into a peaceful kingdom of the very widely separated former enemies:

> And the Lord shall smite *Egypt:*
> he shall smite and heal it:
> and they shall return even to the Lord,
> and he shall be intreated of them,
> and shall heal them.
> In that day there shall be a highway out of *Egypt* to *Assyria,*
> and the *Assyrian* shall some into *Egypt,*
> and the *Egyptian* into *Assyria,*
> and the *Egyptians* shall serve with the Assyrians.
> In that day shall *Israel* be the third
> with *Egypt* and with *Assyria,*
> even a blessing in the midst of the land:
> Whom the Lord of hosts shall bless, saying,
> Blessed be *Egypt my people,*
> and *Assyria the work of my hands,*
> and *Israel mine inheritance.*
>
> (Isaiah 19:22-25.)

This divinely assimilated combination of peoples was also described in a concise overview of the Lord's processes of bringing it about: "For the Lord will have mercy on Jacob, and will yet choose Israel, and set them in their own land: and the strangers shall be joined with them, and they shall cleave to the house of Jacob" (Isaiah 14:1).

The function of the chosen people to bring about these blessed conditions is to be an active, faithful servant: "But thou, Israel, art my servant, Jacob whom I have chosen, the seed of Abraham my friend" (Isaiah 41:8). In the remainder of that chapter, following that declaration, the Lord promised his servant help, protection, and power to overcome enemies, and then proclaimed (in the beginning of the next chapter): "Behold my servant, whom I uphold; mine elect, in whom my soul delighteth; I have put my spirit upon him: he shall bring forth *judgment to the Gentiles*" (Isaiah 42:1). Later on in the same message the Lord continued, "I the Lord have called thee in righteousness, and will hold thine hand, and will keep thee, and give thee for a covenant of the people, for a *light of the Gentiles*" (Isaiah 42:6).

Sometimes there is a combination of functions of prophet, people, and Messiah involved in the prophetic anticipation of the extension of the message and power of salvation to all: "It is a light thing that thou shouldest be my servant to raise up the tribes of Jacob, and to restore the preserved of Israel: I will also give thee for *a light to the Gentiles, that thou mayest be my salvation unto the end of the earth*" (Isaiah 49:3-6). Centuries later, in the temple at Jerusalem, one Simeon, a devout old man waiting for a fulfillment of promise to him, saw in the baby Jesus "*a light to lighten the Gentiles, and the glory of thy people Israel*" (Luke 2:32).

The scriptures show quite explicitly that the chosen people function as messengers and witnesses for the Lord after he has gathered and redeemed them (see Isaiah 43:1, 5, 10, 12, 25, etc.). Elucidation of such functions, along with descriptions of the results of such work, are seen in Isaiah chapter 44. Jacob the servant—Israel the chosen—is assured of seed, of offspring, who shall yet spring up; and then others shall come to them: "One shall say I am the Lord's; and another shall call himself by the name of Jacob; and another shall subscribe with his hand unto the Lord, and surname himself by the name of Israel" (Isaiah 44:1-6).

Everyone who thirsts is invited to partake of the waters, and of the wine and the milk, without money and without price, according to another revelation through Isaiah. The invitation reads in part:

Incline your ear, and come unto me:
hear, and your soul shall live;
and I will make an everlasting covenant with you,
even the sure mercies of David [i.e., salvation by the Savior].
Behold, I have given him for a witness to the people,
a leader and commander to the people.
Behold, thou shalt call a *nation that thou knowest not,*
and *nations that knew not thee* shall run unto thee
because of the Lord thy God,
and for the Holy One of Israel;
for he hath glorified thee.

(Isaiah 55:3-5.)

In the next chapter of Isaiah the Lord assures all that his salvation is near and that the man is blessed "that layeth hold on it," be he the "son of the stranger" who has joined himself to the

Lord, or the former marked slave—"the eunuch"—or of the "outcasts of Israel": "for mine house shall be called an house of prayer for *all people.*" And "the Lord God which gathereth the outcasts of Israel saith, Yet will I gather others to him, beside those that are gathered unto him." (Isaiah 56:1-8.)

The duty of the people of the covenant, the people of the mission, plainly is to "arise" and to "shine," for when their "light is come, and the glory of the Lord is risen upon" them (Isaiah 60:1), then

> the *Gentiles* shall come to thy light,
> and *kings* to the brightness of thy rising.
> Lift up thine eyes round about, and see:
> all they gather themselves together,
> they come to thee:
> thy sons shall come from far,
> and thy daughters shall be nursed at thy side.
> Then thou shalt see, and flow together,
> and thine heart shall fear, and be enlarged;
> because *the abundance of the sea shall be converted* unto
>   thee,
> *the forces of the Gentiles* shall come unto thee.
>   (Isaiah 60:3-5.)

Zechariah later portrayed these same scenes:

> Sing and rejoice, O daughter of Zion:
> for, lo, I come,
> and I will dwell in the midst of thee, saith the Lord.
> And *many nations* shall be joined to the Lord in that day,
> and shall be my people:
> and I will dwell in the midst of thee.
>   (Zechariah 2:10-11.)

And the last prophet of the Old Testament summed it up:

> For from the rising of the sun
> even unto the going down of the same
> my name shall be great *among the Gentiles;*
> and in every place incense shall be offered unto my name,
> and a pure offering:
> for *my name shall be great among the heathen,*
> saith the Lord of hosts.
>   (Malachi 1:11.)

The first writers of the New Testament took up the theme and confirmed it: "This gospel of the kingdom shall be preached *in all the world* for a witness *unto all nations* . . ." (Matthew 24:14; compare Mark 13:10; Luke 24:47). Paul, the Apostle to the Gentiles, was called to implement an important dispensation of it (see Acts 9:15; 11:1-18). He understood clearly that it was intended from the beginning that the blessings of Abraham should come upon the Gentiles (see Galatians 3:7, 14, 26-29; Romans 2:10; 8:15-17; 9:24; 11:13; Ephesians 3:6). Latter-day revelation refreshes and reiterates the charge: "The voice of warning shall be unto all people," and the testimony must again go from the chosen people of the Restoration unto all the world (see D&C 1:4; 84:62; compare also D&C 65:2 and Daniel 2:35). These were the things anticipated by the prophets of the Old Testament. The covenants of old would be established anew and written, not on tablets of stone but in the heart, in the new hearts of the newly chosen people of the Lord (see Ezekiel 16:60-63; 36:26; Jeremiah 31:31-34). All who feel these things in their hearts have what is called a "testimony," and all who are willing-hearted among them go forth to bear it as a mission unto the nations, unto all families of the earth.

9

A Scientific Analysis of Isaiah Authorship

L. La Mar Adams

The disputed authorship of Isaiah is one of the most popular textual biblical issues and appears to be the father of all Old Testament authorship problems of the same nature.

The majority of biblical scholars divide the book of Isaiah into multiple authorship. The problem of identifying authorship for the book and parts of the book is known as the "Isaiah problem." Previously, numerous but unsuccessful approaches have been made toward the solution of this problem.

History of the Isaiah Problem

The so-called Isaiah problem dates back to A.D. 1100, when a Jewish commentator named Moses ben Samuel, Ibn-Gekatilla, denied that Isaiah was the author of certain chapters of the book of Isaiah.[1] Later, in A.D. 1167, Ibn Ezra also questioned the authorship of certain sections of the book of Isaiah.[2] J. C. Doederlein of the Wellhousen school is credited with having given the theory of multiple authorship its major initial support.[3] This theory grew until some scholars claimed that the book of Isaiah was a compilation of works from many authors and many periods of time.[4]

The ancient and formerly unquestioned tradition of the Christian church, inherited earlier from the Jewish tradition, was that the entire book of Isaiah was written by a single author, the prophet Isaiah.[5] Josephus (ca. A.D. 90) stated that King Cyrus read about himself in the prophecies of Isaiah.[6] However, the problem of authorship of the book of Isaiah originated among the Jewish sages and received considerable attention among the higher critics of the Old Testament over a period of several centuries. Those most responsible for the early popularity of the theory in the modern era were the biblical critics from Germany, especially Wellhousen. Scholars who divided the book of Isaiah into multiple authorship were referred to as "divisionists"; those who defended single authorship were referred to as "conservatives." For every conservative scholar today there are eight to ten divisionist scholars.[7] The vast majority of divisionist scholars divide the book of Isaiah into three authorships which they refer to as Isaiah, Deutero-Isaiah, and Trito-Isaiah. Approximately one-third of the divisionists divide the book into two authorships. Several divisionists maintain that the book is a compilation of many different authors from many different periods of time, and this camp is growing rapidly.[8] According to some, little remains of the book of Isaiah which can be attributed to the prophet of the eighth century B.C. In his *Dictionary of the Bible,* John McKenzie claimed:

> Most of the book of Isaiah does not come from the Prophet Isaiah, and even those discourses which are his come in the reports of those who wrote them down from auditions or from memory. The book is a compendium of many types of prophecy from diverse periods.[9]

Edward Young stated that the process of dissection, begun by Bernhard Duhm, probably reached the maximum point of disintegration in the views of Robert Kennett.[10] Charles C. Torrey complained that the paring process, begun with a penknife, was continued with a hatchet until the book had been "chopped into hopeless chunks."[11] An analysis of the divisions postulated by divisionist scholars indicated that there was no agreement between any two of them as to where the division occurred in the book of Isaiah.

The division of the book of Isaiah was followed by authorship division of other Old Testament books by the higher critics, until finally there is no Old Testament book that is not divided into multiple authorship.

In a number of cases, the same evidences, interpreted differently, were given by both divisionists and conservatives in support of their opposing conclusion. Otto Eissfeldt, himself a divisionist, indicated the contradictions in the following quotation:

> That there are many common features both in ideas and linguistic usage between XL-LV and LVI-LXVI, is however also admitted by those who do not believe in the identity of the compilers of the two sections. The differences of opinion on this question itself seggests [sic] that the arguments adduced to decide it are ambiguous and can hence be applied in opposite ways.[12]

Historical Arguments

Fundamental arguments against Isaiah's authorship of the entire book may be classified into three basic types: historical, theoretical, and literary. We will first consider the historical arguments.

It was claimed by divisionists that a prophet is sent to prophesy to the people of his own time and that his predictions do not extend beyond the horizon of his own day. Norman Gottwald claimed:

> When [the prophetic writings are] studied in their context, apart from dogmatic pre-conviction, [it is clear that] no prophet leaped across the centuries and foresaw the specific person Jesus of Nazareth. It is a plain violation of historical context to think that they did so, and in practice those that interpret the prophets as predictors of Jesus obscure the setting in which the prophets functioned.[13]

Historical arguments are often cited by those who advocate multiple authorship. References to historical events such as the conquest of Israel by Assyria,[14] the Babylonian exile,[15] and post-exilic conditions[16] were interpreted by divisionists to have been written after the occurrence of such events.

The classical problem cited by Old Testament critics is the prophecy concerning King Cyrus of Persia, who is mentioned by name in Isaiah chapters 44 and 45. It has been argued that Isaiah, living in the eighth century B.C., could not have written the prophecy, since to do so would have required a projection of more than two centuries into the future. The conservatives have argued that the Prophet Isaiah actually predicted events related to Cyrus and Babylonia. R. K. Harrison observed that the conservative scholars cited other Old Testament prophecies which span future centuries to foretell specific names and events (see 1 Kings 13:1f.; Micah 5:2; Ezekiel 26:2ff.; Zechariah 9:1ff).[17]

Theological Arguments

According to some divisionists, theological concepts such as the majesty of Jehovah in the latter section of the book were fundamentally different than in the first part of the book. Conservatives argue that changes in theological concepts do not imply changes in authorship.

Historical and theoretical arguments have carried relatively little weight with the scholars of the Old Testament, and so the vast majority of the discussion has centered around literary arguments.

Literary Arguments

The most commonly discussed literary aspect of the book of Isaiah is authorship style. Divisionists claim that they see different authorship styles in the different sections of the book. But conservatives have provided extensive rebuttals to the divisionists' arguments. James Smart, a divisionist, summed up the situation on both sides of the issue in the following assertion:

> An honest recognition of the meagerness of the evidence demands of us a suspension of judgment. Yet one commentator after another has proceeded to base his interpretations upon assumptions that have rested on the flimsiest of foundations.[18]

Scientific Approach to Authorship Style

What is a scientific approach to the authorship of a book? Simply stated, it is to search out all available evidence, pro and con, to see where the weight of evidence rests. Often, some of the evidence must be put to an appropriate test to see if it is valid and to determine its weight in relation to other evidence. In fact, some types of evidence outweigh all the others put together.

Where would we start looking for a scientific approach to an analysis of the authorship style in the book of Isaiah? Would we begin by asking what evidence exists? In response to these questions, a survey was made several years ago of all available literature on the so-called Isaiah problem.[19] Claims made by all the various authors were tabulated into various categories of pro and con in relation to the claim for single authorship of the book of Isaiah. Some divisionists assert that no literary evidence exists for authorship unity of the book. One German critic, Georg Fohrer,[20] claimed that all literary evidence points to multiple authorship. The divisionists emphasize the literary differences between the various sections of Isaiah, and conservatives the similarities.

The above-mentioned research, which we will now examine, involved a computer and thirty-five researchers and associates across several disciplines at Brigham Young University over a period of three years. It was designed to test the validity of claims made by the biblical scholars.

Computerized Style Analysis

Since divisionists have claimed that authorship styles of speaking and writing vary significantly in the different sections of the book of Isaiah, the literary elements given as evidence were examined with the help of the computer to test the validity of these claims. Claims made by the conservative scholars were also tested.

Analysis of authorship style of this nature involves comparing the rates of usage of literary elements in one section of the book with rates of usage in another to determine if the rates of usage are the same in both sections. The method used compares the rates by means of computerized statistical procedures. However, the type of statistical analysis is determined by the type of literary elements being analyzed and the manner in which they are to be analyzed. For example, one cannot select just any literary element to compare authorship styles between two texts, since many literary elements are used at different rates and in different ways by any given author from one context to another. If a young man writes a letter to his sweetheart, it is expected to contain certain types of words and expressions not expected to be found in a letter the same young man may write in protesting some government action. Therefore, some claims made by biblical scholars, conservative or divisionist, may be valid but are not evidence of either single or multiple authorship. This was found to be the case when many claims of the biblical scholars were put to the test. For example, on one hand, the use of war terminology claimed by Yehuda Radday to be evidence of multiple authorship was found to be based on an invalid assumption.[21] On the other hand, many of the conjunction words claimed by the conservative scholar Letitia D. Jefferys to be evidence of single authorship were found to be unsupportive of her claims.[22] These two examples also serve as instances of the use of literary variables which do not serve as evidence in an authorship study of this type.

In a valid study, the literary variables examined must be the type that identify authorship styles unique to the author. The best kind of literary element for this type of analysis consists of habit-prone parts of speech. Identification of habit-prone types of speech, particularly those that are used subconsciously, is extremely difficult, especially in the English language. However, in classical Hebrew there is a prefix characteristic which makes it possible to identify many habit-prone parts of speech by use of computerized statistical analysis. This type of prefix is referred to as a "function prefix." The use of certain words and prefixes is influenced more by the context of the writing than by the authorship style. Pronominal, verbal, and participial prefixes are judged to be too contextually oriented for authorship identification. Therefore, function prefixes include all prefixes except those which are pronominal, verbal, and participial.

The purposes of this study were twofold: (1) to statistically analyze the validity of the claims and the supportive materials for and against the unity of Isaiah authorship as made by biblical scholars in the available literature, and (2) to provide a valid computerized statistical approach in determining authorship of the book of Isaiah.

Procedures

Computer programs were written to obtain data for analyzing the validity of claims made by scholars concerning the Isaiah problem. The Hebrew text was used for analysis, including the complete Hebrew text of the book of Isaiah, and random samples from eleven additional Old Testament books were used. (The eleven additional books, selected by stratified random sampling, were Amos, Jeremiah, Ezekiel, Hosea, Micah, Habakkuk, Zechariah, Daniel, Ezra, Malachi, and Nehemiah. These books served as Hebrew control texts for comparison with the book of Isaiah.) The book of Isaiah was divided into the various sections suggested by divisionists. The major sets of divisions analyzed for authorship style consisted of the following:

1. The commonly used twofold: Chapters 1-39 and 40-66, the so-called Deutero-Isaiah.
2. The more popular threefold division: Chapters 1-39, 40-55, and 56-66, the so-called Trito-Isaiah.
3. Radday's division: Chapters 1-12, 13-23, 24-35, 36-39 (omitted by Radday), 40-48, 49-57, and 58-66.
4. Driver's division: Chapters 1-12, 13-23, 24-27, 28-33, 34-35, 36-39, 40-48, 49-55, 56-62, and 63-66.[23]

This study is the most extensive to date. Specialists in the areas of Semitics, languages, statistics, and computer science were involved. Over seventy different types of stylistic elements were examined, and several hundred linguistic variables were analyzed. The major analysis consisted of comparing the rate of usage of literary variables with authorship styles across the different sections of Isaiah. Similar comparisons were made within and between the eleven Old Testament control texts and the book of Isaiah.

Statistical Results

Among all the statistical elements examined in this study, the function prefix provided the most valid approach. The book of Isaiah has a surprisingly large number of function prefixes indicating single authorship. Out of 36 different prefixes and prefix combinations examined in the Hebrew text, 24 occurred in the book of Isaiah. The accompanying table shows the usage frequency of 18 of these 24 function prefixes. Although each of the 18 prefixes was used in both sections in the book of Isaiah (chapters 1 to 39 and 40 to 66), some of the prefixes were not found in a number of the control texts.

It is evident from the last two columns in the table (Isaiah A and Isaiah B) that the rates of usage for a number of prefixes show a similarity between the two Isaiah texts that is peculiar to the book of Isaiah and contrasts markedly with the control texts. For example, both Isaiah sections have a rate of 2 (equivalent to .02 per 50 prefixes) for the prefix *bet-mem* (shown as BM in the table)

Average Frequencies* per Prefix Block from Old Testament Sample Texts and the Two Sections of the Book of Isaiah for Certain Function Prefixes

Abbreviations for the 11 Sample Texts, Isaiah 1-39, and Isaiah 40-66

Prefixes	AM	DN	EZ	HB	HS	JR	MC	ML	NH	ZC	ZK	Isa.A	Isa.B
B	920	325	400	733	900	750	966	600	200	625	950	688	676
E	1120	425	925	700	233	1125	566	700	1225	1475	800	752	467
K	120	25	50	233	633	50	300	33	200	175	50	231	219
L	500	625	825	833	900	850	666	500	500	400	375	700	863
M	360	100	325	500	333	300	666	533	475	150	375	446	521
V	1700	1700	1425	1800	1833	1650	1633	2266	1650	1950	1650	1834	1884
BM	00	00	00	00	00	00	00	00	00	00	00	2	2
EK	00	00	00	00	00	00	00	00	00	00	00	1	2
EM	00	00	00	00	00	00	00	00	00	00	00	4	6
LM	00	00	25	33	00	00	00	00	00	00	00	2	6
ME	20	00	25	00	00	00	00	00	25	00	75	15	10
MN	40	50	125	00	00	00	00	00	50	00	50	11	2
VB	80	50	125	00	66	100	33	166	175	00	150	68	80
VE	40	125	75	100	00	75	33	166	200	25	150	76	56
VEM	00	00	00	00	00	00	00	00	25	00	00	1	2
VK	00	50	00	00	66	00	66	33	00	25	00	15	47
VL	00	75	50	00	00	50	00	00	200	150	00	68	67
VM	80	50	125	00	33	00	33	00	50	00	00	56	73

*Average frequencies were multiplied by 100 for statistical applications.

compared to .00 for each of the control texts. (The .00 indicates that this function prefix was not used in the control text.)

Another example of uniqueness in the book of Isaiah may be observed in the usage rate of the prefix *vav-lamed* (VL in the table) in the English text. Isaiah 19:24 concludes with a description of a condition in the millennial era: "In that day shall Israel be the third part with Egypt *and with* Assyria." In this phrase, the Hebrew prefix *vav-lamed* is rendered *"and with."* This prefix combination may also be translated as *"and to."* In Isaiah 60:9 we read the phrase "to bring thy sons . . . unto the name of the Lord thy God, *and to* the Holy One of Israel." This has reference to the gathering of exiled Israel in the latter days.

The usage rate for *vav-lamed* is unique to the book of Isaiah, occurring approximately .68 times for every 50 function prefixes in Isaiah A and .67 times per 50 prefixes in Isaiah B, compared to a zero rate (that is, almost never) for such books as Amos, Micah, and Ezekiel. Usage of this prefix occurs at a high rate of 2 per 50 prefixes in the book of Nehemiah, as exemplified in Nehemiah 2:16: "Neither had I as yet told it to the Jews, *nor to* the priests, *nor to* the nobles, *nor to* the rulers, *nor to* the rest that did the work."

One example of a function prefix which serves as an idiomatic part of speech is the one which translates into "and in this." The rate of usage of this phrase was found to be constant across the different sections of the book of Isaiah, in contrast to the rates of usage in other Old Testament texts. This phrase and the other function prefixes in the table had usage rates so peculiar to the book of Isaiah that single authorship was strongly evident.

In this phase of the analysis we drew heavily on the statistical expertise of Dr. Alvin Rencher, presently chairman of the BYU Statistics Department. We found that the authorship style was more consistent in the book of Isaiah than in any of the other Old Testament books we examined. Some otherwise conservative scholars who have ascribed the book of Isaiah to the prophet Isaiah claim that the historical chapters 36 to 39 were written by another author. However, the results of this study indicate that chapters 36 to 39 are not to be denied the prophet Isaiah. Even the ten verses by King Hezekiah in chapter 28 may have been written in the original records by Isaiah. There is some evidence that a later transcriber abridged the text. However, such alterations were evidently not extensive enough to camouflage the literary style of the original author.

Summary and Conclusions

The statistical results in this study do not support the divisionists' claim that little or no evidence exists for unity of the book of Isaiah. To the contrary, the results strongly support single authorship of the book. The divisions of the book most often claimed to have been written by different authors were found to be more similar to each other in authorship style than to any of the control group of eleven other Old Testament books. The book of Isaiah also exhibited greater internal consistency than any of the other books when authorship style was analyzed.

These results do not exclude the possibility that minor changes in the text have been made by scribes and editors since the time of its origin. However, the evidence indicates that in spite of such possible changes, an overall style has been retained as measured by the literary variables examined. The results of this research bear witness that the book of Isaiah has a literary unity characteristic of a single author. These results, therefore, confirm the claims made in the Book of Mormon and the New Testament by later prophets and by the Savior that Isaiah was the author of the book bearing his name.

Previous Attempts at Statistical Analysis

Previous attempts at computerized statistical analysis of the book of Isaiah were made by two different researchers, Yehuda Radday[24] and Asa Kasher.[25] Both of these researchers independently concluded that the book of Isaiah was written by multiple authors. Radday's work was based on an inappropriate assumption: he assumed that a difference in the usage of one type of word (such as war terminology) from one section or prophecy to another was an indication of a difference in authorship. To demonstrate the invalidity of his method, we applied Radday's procedures to a text known to have been written by Thomas Carlisle. The result was a false conclusion that part of Carlisle's text was written by another author.[26]

Kasher's approach was likewise analyzed and found to be

based on inappropriate assumptions. I have corresponded extensively with these two Israeli researchers, and they are aware of the problems in their research.

The Need for Multiple Authorship

Why do most biblical scholars insist on multiple authorship for the book of Isaiah? Evidently the reason lies in the fact that the scholars do not believe that a prophet can prophesy beyond his own time period. George Robinson summarized the arguments postulated by divisionists against futuristic prophecy:

> The fundamental axiom of criticism is the dictum that a prophet always spoke out of a definite historical situation to the present needs of the people among whom he lives, and that a definite historical situation shall be pointed out for each prophecy. This fundamental postulate . . . underlies all modern criticism of O. T. prophecy.[27]

Harrison claimed that argument concerning prophecy was embarrassing to critical scholars:

> On the basis of their insistence that there was no predictive element in prophecy, they tried to dismiss the problem or more commonly, to avert the critical gaze from it.[28]

Why is it that the critics do not believe in the type of revelation that allows prophets to give futuristic prophecy? The Savior himself answered this question:

> He that believeth not is condemned. . . . And this is the condemnation, that light is come into the world, and men loved darkness rather than light, because their deeds were evil. For every one that doeth evil hateth the light, neither cometh to the light, lest his deeds should be reproved. (John 3:18-20.)

Denial by critics that certain prophecies in the book of Isaiah were written by the prophet himself fulfill, at least in part, an ancient prophecy ascribed to Isaiah in an apocryphal work entitled the "Ascension of Isaiah" (3:30-31):

> For there will be great jealousy in the last days; for everyone will say what is pleasing in his own eye. And they will make of none effect the prophecy of the prophets which were before me, and these my visions also, will they make of none effect in order to speak after the impulse of their own hearts.[29]

We are living in a day when the prophecies of Isaiah are being fulfilled. These evidences that the book of Isaiah was written by the prophet Isaiah help us understand his prophecies. They also serve as an additional witness to the truthfulness of the Book of Mormon and New Testament statements from prophets and the Savior concerning the words of Isaiah. Together they all help to bring us closer to the Lord. If we are to go where Isaiah goes, we will need to know what Isaiah knows. The more we read the words of Isaiah, the more we will become like him, the other prophets, and the Savior.

Notes

1. Edward J. Young, *An Introduction to the Old Testament* (Grand Rapids, Mich.: William B. Eerdman's Publishing Company, 1949), p. 199.

2. George A. Buttrick et al., eds., *The Interpreter's Bible,* vol. 5 (New York: Abingdon Press, 1956), p. 382.

3. R. K. Harrison, *Introduction to the Old Testament* (Grand Rapids, Mich.: William B. Eerdman's Publishing Company, 1969), p. 763.

4. John L. McKenzie, *Dictionary of the Bible* (Milwaukee: Bruce Publishing Company, 1965), p. 397.

5. Sidney B. Sperry, *The Voice of Israel's Prophets* (Salt Lake City: Deseret Book Company, 1961), p. 84; Larry L. Adams, "A Statistical Analysis of the Book of Isaiah in Relation to the Isaiah Problem" (Ph.D. dissertation, Brigham Young University, 1972), pp. 10-11.

6. Flavius Josephus, *Josephus: Complete Works,* trans. William Whiston (Grand Rapids, Mich.: Kregel Publications, 1960), *The Antiquities of the Jews,* XI:1:1f.

7. Adams, pp. 19-23.

8. Ibid.; also Georg Fohrer, *Introduction to the Old Testament* (New York: Abingdon Press, 1967), p. 385.

9. McKenzie, p. 387.

10. Edward J. Young, *Who Wrote Isaiah?* (Grand Rapids, Mich.: William B. Eerdman's Publishing Company, 1958), p. 20.

11. Charles C. Torrey, *The Second Isaiah* (New York: Scribners, 1928), p. 13.

12. Otto Eissfeldt, *The Old Testament: An Introduction,* trans. Peter R. Ackroyd (Oxford: Basil Blackwell, 1966), p. 342.

13. Norman K. Gottwald, *A Light to the Nations: An Introduction to the Old Testament* (New York: Harper, 1959), p. 275.

14. Aage Bentzen, *Introduction to the Old Testament*, 2 vols. (Copenhagen: Gads Forlag, 1949), 2:107.

15. Christopher R. North, *The Second Isaiah* (Oxford: Clarendon Press, 1964), p. 3.

16. Claus Westermann, *Isaiah 40-66* (Philadelphia: Westminster Press, 1969), pp. 296-99.

17. Harrison, p. 765.

18. James D. Smart, *History and Theology in Second Isaiah* (Philadelphia: Westminster Press, 1965), p. 30.

19. Adams, pp. 10-42.

20. Fohrer, p. 385.

21. Adams, pp. 90-92.

22. Ibid., pp. 107-18.

23. L. La Mar Adams and Alvin C. Rencher, "A Computer Analysis of the Isaiah Authorship Problem," *BYU Studies* 15 (Autumn 1974):97.

24. Yehuda T. Radday, "The Unity of Isaiah: Computerized Test in Linguistics" (unpublished report, Israel Institute of Technology, 1970).

25. Asa Kasher, "The Book of Isaiah: Characterization of Authors by Morphological Data Processing" (unpublished essay, Department of Mathematics, Bar-Ilan University, Ramat-Gan, Israel, 1970).

26. Adams, pp. 93-95.

27. George L. Robinson, "Isaiah," in *The International Standard Bible Encyclopedia*, ed. James Orr, 5 vols. (Grand Rapids, Mich.: William B. Eerdman's Publishing Company, 1960), 3:1505.

28. Harrison, p. 776.

29. L. La Mar Adams, *The Living Message of Isaiah* (Salt Lake City: Deseret Book Company, 1981), p.111.

10

Isaiah Variants in the Book of Mormon

John A. Tvedtnes

Of the 478 verses in the Book of Mormon quoted from the book of Isaiah, 201 agree with the King James reading while 207 show variations. Some 58 are paraphrased and 11 others are variants and/or paraphrases. It is to the variants that we will give our attention here.

Two factors led to my study of the Isaiah variants in the Book of Mormon. The first was a paper written by a friend of mine and now widely circulated as "evidence" against the Book of Mormon. It is essentially a statistical analysis of the frequency of changes made in the Isaiah passages in the Book of Mormon, and it concludes that because there are more such changes earlier on than later, this indicates that Joseph Smith wearied of making alterations as time went by. My objections to the study are basically twofold: First, some of the changes made by the Prophet fit the reading found in some ancient versions of Isaiah. Secondly, the study did not take into account that some of the changes were not in the first edition of the Book of Mormon but were added later. I contend that these changes have no bearing on Joseph Smith's translation. Moreover, many of them were stylistic or grammatical, such as the change from "which" to "who" or "whom" when the referent is human. To my way of thinking, it makes more sense to examine substantive differences between the texts of the King James and Book of Mormon versions of Isaiah.

The second impetus for my study came from an assignment given me to serve on the Book of Mormon Hebrew translation committee. One of my specific tasks was to examine all of the biblical quotes in the Book of Mormon to determine what changes, if any, would need to be made to the Hebrew translations of those books when the passages were incorporated into the translation. It was my feeling that we should try to render the translated Book of Mormon passages into the form in which Nephi and other Book of Mormon writers would have known them from the brass plates of Laban, which they took with them.

It was first necessary to identify all of the variants and paraphrases from Isaiah found in the Book of Mormon.[1] To do this I read and reread each of the texts several times, checked out the cross-references, and looked up the key words in exhaustive concordances of the Bible and of the Book of Mormon. My wife and I then proceeded to compare the King James (KJV) and Book of Mormon (BM) texts of Isaiah, looking for differences. I read aloud from the BM while she followed in the KJV, and we marked the differences in green ink in a special copy of the Book of Mormon. Next, we did the same thing with the BM and the original 1830 edition, noting any differences in red ink. We used blue ink to mark differences between it and the RLDS version and some few items I was able to obtain from the handwritten BM manuscripts.

The next step was to look up all of the variant verses in different versions of the book of Isaiah: the Hebrew Massoretic text (MT), the Hebrew scrolls found at Qumran (notably IQIsa, which contains all sixty-six chapters), the Aramaic Targumim (T), the Peshitta (P), the Septuagint (LXX) or Greek translation, the Old Latin (OL) and Vulgate (V), and the Isaiah passages quoted in the New Testament. I also read dozens of articles and books written by the top experts on Isaiah and gleaned from them leads to other manuscript variants, such as those found in quotations by the early Church Fathers and other little-known documents.

To be frank, I did not expect to find the volume of support for the BM version of Isaiah that I did in fact discover. I knew enough about ancient manuscripts to realize that there were oftentimes several different versions, no two of which agreed completely with one another. In such cases it is impossible to know which version, if any, is the "original." It was therefore necessary to allow for errors on the brass plates of Laban from which the BM Isaiah passages were taken.

I have classified the variants according to seventeen different types. Some of these classifications are favorable to the BM versions, while others favor the KJV. Still others favor neither. In the listing below, those favorable to BM are marked +, those neutral =, and those unfavorable −.

Type of Variation	*Frequency*	*Relation to BM*
1. BM superior to KJV as a translation from MT Hebrew	4	+
2. Version support for BM	36	+
3. Evidence of ancient scribal error favoring BM	13	+
4. Evidence that BM is from a more ancient text than MT	1	+
5. Singular-plural distinctions		
a. Version support for BM	5	+
b. Other (perhaps all due to abbreviation)	6	=
6. BM and KJV equally valid translations from MT	18	=
7. BM and KJV/MT disagree, where some other versions also disagree without supporting either	8	=
8. Textual additions found elsewhere in Bible (2 in Isaiah)	4	−
9. Deletion of KJV italicized words in BM[2] (8 returned after 1830)	59	=
10. Change of KJV italicized words		
a. Not affecting meaning	35	=
b. Affecting meaning	2	−
11. BM variations from KJV (=MT) without explanation	43	−
12. Uncorrected BM scribal/printer errors[3]	29	N/A

13.	BM scribal/printer errors subsequently corrected	17	N/A
14.	Attempts at updating KJV language in BM	25	N/A
15.	Changes in post-1830 editions of BM (mostly for style or spelling)	47	N/A
16.	Internal variations in BM Isaiah passages	Not counted here	
17.	Paraphrases	Not counted here	

Of the 234 variants rated, 59 are +, 126 are =, and 49 are −. That is, there are more favoring the Book of Mormon than the KJV, while most favor neither.

Having briefly reviewed the procedure of this study and some of its statistical results, I want now to turn to an examination of some examples of the variants.[4] The examples presented here have been chosen on the basis of the ease with which I can explain them to non-Semiticists and the favorable light which they shed on the Book of Mormon translation.

Two terms which should be introduced here for the non-linguist are "dittography" and "haplography." The first refers to the repetition of words (e.g., "I went to *the the* store"), while the second refers to the dropping of a word or words because it/they resemble(s) what immediately precedes or follows. These types of mistakes are scribal errors and are common occurrences in hand-written documents, notably when the scribe is fatigued. Let us compare Isaiah 2:6 with 2 Nephi 12:6:

> KJV "Therefore" is extended in BM to read "Therefore, O Lord." There was probably an abbreviation, *k"y*, read by MT as *ky* ("therefore") and by BM as *ky Yhwh* ("therefore, O Lord"). That this was the case is evidenced by the fact that there must have been Hebrew versions reading *ky Y'qb* ("therefore, O Jacob") and *ky Ysr'1* ("therefore, O Israel"), with words beginning with the same letters, for different LXX manuscripts so translate in the Greek.

Isaiah 2:11 compared with 2 Nephi 12:11:

> BM adds to the beginning, "And it shall come to pass that . . ." IQIsa and LXX add the conjunction "and," in partial agree-

ment. MT probably lost the conjunction (Hebrew *w-*) by haplography, for it is the last consonant of verse 10.

Isaiah 2:14 compared with 2 Nephi 12:14:

BM adds information to the KJV text in verses 12-14. In each case, the additional information enhances the parallels found in the poetry. In verse 14, for example, BM adds "and upon all the nations which are lifted up, and upon every people." Obviously, the "nations" and "people" parallel each other. In order to see the complete list of parallels between words such as "nation," "people," "hills," and "trees," note verses 12-15.

In a number of passages, BM adds the conjunction "and" to the text of KJV and finds confirmation in at least some of the versions. The examples of this are listed below, along with the versions which support BM.

Isaiah 3:9	=2 Nephi 13:9	IQIsa, LXX, Peshitta, 1 Targum
Isaiah 3:14	=2 Nephi 13:14	LXX
Isaiah 3:26	=2 Nephi 13:26	LXX
Isaiah 48:8	=2 Nephi 20:8	IQIsa
Isaiah 48:13	=1 Nephi 20:13	IQIsa, LXX, S, Peshitta
Isaiah 48:14	=1 Nephi 20:14	IQIsa
Isaiah 50:9	=2 Nephi 7:9	LXX
Isaiah 48:22	=1 Nephi 20:22	IQIsa (BM adds "also")
Isaiah 51:18	=2 Nephi 8:18	LXX (BM "and" replaces KJV "there is")
Isaiah 48:5	=1 Nephi 20:5	BM adds "and" to KJV in a place where MT has the conjunction but KJV did not translate it!

Isaiah 2:5 compared with 2 Nephi 12:5:

At the end, BM adds, "yea, come, for ye have all gone astray, every one to his wicked ways." The wording is found in Isaiah 53:6 and is thus something one might expect in the book. The Hebrew behind BM would have begun with the words *b'w ky*, "come, for . . ." Compare the next-to-last word of the same verse, *b'wr* ("in light"), and the first word of verse 6, *ky* ("for"), which may have influenced the dropping of the BM wording by haplography in MT.

Isaiah 2:16 compared with 2 Nephi 12:16:

> KJV: "And upon all the ships of Tarshish"
>
> BM: "And upon all the ships of the sea,
>   and upon all the ships of Tarshish"

Here, BM adds a line not found in KJV. Interestingly, LXX reads "And upon every ship of the sea, and upon all views of pleasant ships," with the last part paralleling KJV/BM "and upon all pleasant pictures." The Greek *talassa,* "sea," resembles the word Tarshish. But both the Targum and the Vulgate have "sea" with LXX instead of Tarshish. The matter is a very complex one, for which a complete discussion cannot be included here. BM appears to have included the versions of both MT and LXX/T/V. MT could have dropped the nearly identical second line by haplography.

Isaiah 2:20 compared with 2 Nephi 12:20:

> KJV: "they   made each one for himself"
>
> BM: "he   hath made   for himself"

MT reads literally, "which they made for him." Most LXX manuscripts follow MT with the plural verb, but delete the dative "for him." LXX_A and Vulgate have the singular verb, like BM. IQIsa is torn at this point, but there is evidence that it kept the plural verb, adding a new subject, "his fingers" (only the last of the word remains on the damaged scroll). The previous verb in the same verse is in the singular, so we should expect the same here, rather than the plural of MT. Moreover, the forms *'śh* ("he made") and *'św* ("they made") anciently would have both been written alike, *'s,* with the suffixes being unwritten vowels (Hebrew originally being written without vowels, which were not added until the early part of the Christian era).

Isaiah 3:1 compared with 2 Nephi 13:1:

The problem found in this verse is known to biblical scholars, who generally consider the text to be corrupt (the New English Bible deletes the problematic passage). KJV speaks of "the stay and the staff" but then goes on to mention the "stay of bread" and the "stay of water." The word translated "stay" from MT is *mš'n,* while its feminine counterpart, *mš'nh,* is translated "staff." The occurrence of the latter but once in MT/KJV destroys a parallel (probably caused by dropping the feminine singular suffix) which is corrected in BM.

Isaiah 3:10 compared with 2 Nephi 13:10:

> KJV: "to   the righteous"
>
> BM: "unto the righteous"

While there is no difference in meaning here, BM nevertheless seems to be stressing the preposition. Curiously, there is no preposition at this point in MT, though one would expect it. It is there, however, in IQIsa (as a superscript) and the Peshitta (which also has the plural, thus confirming BM's "them" vs. KJV's "him" which follows). The parallel word, "wicked," in the same verse, does have the preposition in MT, and we should expect it to be here also. We thus have evidence of the antiquity of the text from which BM came, as compared with MT.

Isaiah 3:26 compared with 2 Nephi 13:26:

> KJV: "and she   being desolate"
>
> BM: "and she shall be   desolate"

Isaiah 6:12 compared with 2 Nephi 16:12:

> KJV: "and there   be a great forsaking"
>
> BM: "for there shall be a great forsaking"

In these two cases, MT has a finite verb which was not so translated by KJV but which is reflected in BM. Thus BM better fits MT in these instances than does KJV.

Isaiah 5:30 compared with 2 Nephi 15:30:

> KJV: "if one look"
>
> BM: "if they look"

In English, the words "one" and "they" are both used to express an indefinite subject; while the MT has the verb in the singular, it could be understood collectively. (In Isaiah 8:22, the same singular form occurs in MT but is translated as "they shall look" by KJV, in a passage parallel to this one.) But LXX has a plural verb here, agreeing with BM.

Isaiah 9:3 (MT 9:2) compared with 2 Nephi 19:3:

> KJV: "and not increased the nation"
>
> BM: "and   increased the nation"

Jewish scholars of the MT sometimes realized that a mistake was present in the biblical text. But since it was forbidden to alter the sacred scriptures, they left the error as a *Ketib* ("that which is written"), while adding a footnoted *Qere* ("that which is read") to be vocalized in reading the text. In this passage, the *Ketib* of MT has the negative particle, while the *Qere* deletes it, as do twenty Hebrew manuscripts, all of which substitute the word *lw* (for *l'*, which is pronounced the same), "for him." Compare the same expression in Job 12:23 and Isaiah 26:15, both of which are like BM.

Isaiah 9:9 (MT 9:8) compared with 2 Nephi 19:9:

There are many instances of singular-plural differences between the KJV and BM texts. One of the classic examples is found in this passage, where KJV has "inhabitant" and BM reads plural "inhabitants." MT has the singular word, which, however, can often have a collective meaning in Hebrew. As in a number of the other examples of this type found in the study, BM is supported by LXX, which also has the plural. And like other examples, we have here the distinct possibility of a Hebrew abbreviation being read as singular by MT and as plural on the brass plates of Laban. The abbreviation may well have been *w-yw″s̆*, which is the very form found at this point in IQIsa! In any event, the sole difference between the singular and plural construct forms of this word would be the addition of the letter *-y* to the end of the plural. This smallest of all Hebrew letters could easily have been lost from the text.

Isaiah 10:29 compared with 2 Nephi 20:29:

KJV "Ramah" (MT *Rmh*) is rendered "Ramath" in BM. This would be the more ancient form of the name, with the old feminine *-ath* suffix which, in later (usually even biblical) Hebrew disappeared in the pausal form of the noun. Compare verse 28, where both KJV and BM have the name "Aiath," with the same feminine ending. This is particularly interesting, since it is *'yt* in MT, but was written as *'yh̆* in IQIsa, with the *-t* suffix apparently added as an afterthought (it is in superscription), following a writing which shows later pronunciation. That is, IQIsa originally wrote it as "Aiah"—as MT wrote "Ramah" —and later added a superscript letter to show the older form "Aiath," possibly copying an older manuscript. This provides evidence that the brass plates are from an older source than MT.

Isaiah 13:3 compared with 2 Nephi 23:3:

KJV: "for mine anger, even   them that rejoice
        in my highness"

BM: "for mine anger is not upon them that rejoice
         in my highness"

MT reads *l-'py 'lyzy g'wty*, literally "to/for mine anger, the rejoicers of my highness." Both KJV and MT are gibberish and require some correction. We probably have here a case of double haplography. To illustrate, let us reproduce the Hebrew of MT and a Hebrew translation of BM:

MT: 1- 'py   'lyzy g'wty

BM: l' 'py 'l 'lyzy g'wty

The MT scribe or a predecessor has—perhaps after a long, tiring day of work—made two deletions here. First, he deleted the Hebrew letter *aleph* (transliterated ') from the negative particle, resulting in the preposition *l-*. Because the earliest Hebrew writing has no spaces to divide words, the mistake would have been easily made. The second deletion involved the preposition *'l* ("upon"). Both of these cases of haplography occurred because of the proximity of other identical alphabetical elements to those being deleted. It is true that in biblical Hebrew we would normally expect *'yn* instead of *l'* as the negative particle in nonverbal sentences such as this. However, the Bible has many examples of such a use for *l'*, four of which occur in Isaiah (27:11; 37:19; 53:2; and 55:8).

Isaiah 13:22 compared with 2 Nephi 23:22:

BM adds to the end of the verse, "For I will destroy her speedily; yea, for I will be merciful unto my people, but the wicked shall perish." There is partial confirmation in the versions. LXX adds, "quickly shall it be done, and shall not be delayed," while IQIsa adds "more (still, yet)." It is possible that MT dropped this verse ending by haplography. The portion added in BM would begin with the Hebrew word *ky*, "for," which happens to be the initial word in the next verse (14:1). Moreover, 14:1 is not a logical successor to 13:22 without the BM addition, which introduces the subject of the Lord's mercy toward Israel.

Isaiah 14:2 compared with 2 Nephi 24:2:

After KJV's "to their place," BM adds, "yea, from far unto the ends of the earth; and they shall return to their lands of promise." MT has only "to their place," finding agreement in LXX and Targum Codex Reuchlinianus. However, BM has support from some of the versions, such as Bibliotheque Nationale Ms.

1325 (reading "to their land") and IQIsa ("to their land and to their place"). Note that verse 1 has "to their own land," which may have influenced the dropping of the BM portion in MT. Also, immediately after the BM addition, MT/KJV has "and the house of Israel shall possess them in the land of the Lord." Here, too, we have "land" and also *byt* ("house"), a word which resembles *bryt* ("covenant"), possibly the "promise" of the BM passage. (Cf. the use of *bryt* in the promise of land to Abraham in Genesis 17:7-10; Psalm 105:8-11.)

Isaiah 14:3 compared with 2 Nephi 24:3:

KJV reads "the day," while BM reads "that day." Though MT agrees with KJV, there are some Hebrew manuscripts which add *h-hw'*, "that." (The full story behind the changes in vss. 3-4 requires a considerable background in Hebrew syntax on the part of the reader and is therefore not detailed here. It is nevertheless of interest that it provides further evidence of the authenticity of the Book of Mormon's source—the brass plates of Laban—as an ancient document.)

Isaiah 14:32 compared with 2 Nephi 24:32:

KJV: "What shall one then answer the messengers . . . ?"

BM: "What shall   then answer the messengers . . . ?"

BM makes "messengers" the subject here. The Hebrew verb is singular in MT, but is plural in IQIsa, LXX, and T, thus agreeing with BM (though all have *mlky*, "kings of," instead of *ml'ky*, "messengers of").

Isaiah 48:11 compared with 1 Nephi 20:11:

KJV: "for how should   my name   be polluted?"

BM: "for I will not suffer my name to be polluted"

While KJV finds support in the third-person conjugation of MT, OL, and LXX (the latter having the word "name," which is not present in the Hebrew text), the majority of the versions back the BM by having the verb in the first person (IQIsa, V, and one Targum [while another agrees with MT]. See Ezekiel 39:7; compare Ezekiel 20:9.

Isaiah 48:14 compared with 1 Nephi 20:14:

After the word "things," BM adds "unto them." The addition also appears in LXX. The Hebrew behind BM would read *'lh 'lhm*, literally "these unto them" (with "things" being understood—actually unnecessary—in the Hebrew). MT evidently dropped the second word by haplography because it resembled the first. This example also provides evidence that BM derives from an older text than MT (i.e., the brass plates).

Isaiah 49:1 compared with 1 Nephi 21:1:

BM adds a preface to the KJV verse. Because the preface is in chiasmus, a poetic style used in biblical Hebrew wherein parallel lines form an "X" shape when diagrammed, it is good evidence of the authenticity of the account on the brass plates, even though there is no support from the versions. The preface may be outlined as follows:

And again:

A Hearken,
  B O ye house of Israel,
    C All ye that are broken off and driven out
      D Because of the wickedness of the pastors of my people;
    C′ Yea, all ye that are broken off, that are scattered abroad,
  B′ Who are of my people, O house of Israel.
A′ Listen, O isles, unto me.

The Hebrew of this addition would begin with the word šmʻw, "hearken," which also begins the section to follow. The loss of the preface in MT was probably due to haplography because of the resemblance of the two parts beginning with the same word.

Isaiah 50:2 compared with 2 Nephi 7:2:

KJV: "their fish   stinketh, because there is no water,
                            and   dieth for thirst"

BM: "and their fish to stink   because the   waters
                        are dried up, and they die   of thirst"

From the perspective of the English, there seems to be no real justification for BM to reword this passage. But the Hebrew is again helpful. There are, in fact, two variants for the first verb in this passage, as found in ancient texts:

| MT (= V) | tbʼš̌ | "shall stink" |
| IQIsa (= LXX) | tybš̌ | "shall dry up" |

BM has both of these meanings, deriving from words which closely resemble one another. It is likely that the other early

Hebrew versions lost one or the other of the original two verbs by haplography.

Isaiah 51:9 compared with 2 Nephi 8:9:

BM deletes from KJV the words "in the generations of old." Some Hebrew manuscripts give partial support by deleting the word "generations."

Isaiah 51:15 compared with 2 Nephi 8:15:

KJV: "his name" (Hebrew šmw)

BM: "my name" (Hebrew šmy)

The two letters forming the suffix for pronominal possession look very much alike in Hebrew and are frequently confused in later manuscripts. This would indicate that the error is in MT, not BM (where the 600 B.C. date would preclude confusing the letters, which at that time were not alike). Support derives from LXX, which reads "my name."

Isaiah 54:15 compared with 3 Nephi 22:15:

KJV: "shall . . . gather together"

BM: "shall . . . gather together against thee"

LXX adds "to thee," thus confirming BM. The addition agrees with the rest of the verse, reading, "whosoever shall gather together against thee . . ."

It has long been my contention that the best scientific evidence for the Book of Mormon is not archaeological or historical in nature, as important as these may be, but rather linguistic. This is because we have before us a printed text which can be subjected to linguistic analysis and comparison with the language spoken in the kingdom of Judah at the time of Lehi.

One of the more remarkable linguistic evidences for the authenticity of the Book of Mormon as a translation from an ancient text lies in the Isaiah variants found in it. The examples given here, though sketchy, are presented to offer some of that evidence to all those who seriously inquire after the origins of the Book of Mormon.

Notes

1. At that time I was unaware that others had done a similar work. However, inasmuch as I was able to discover a larger list than heretofore recognized, I feel justified in the approach taken.

2. Words which appear in italics in the King James Bible were added to make sense of the English translation and do not exist in the Hebrew text from which KJV derives.

3. The items marked N/A ("not applicable") do not bear on Joseph Smith's translation, but only on later printed versions of the Book of Mormon, and in some few cases on the manuscript prepared by Oliver Cowdery from dictation.

4. It is not possible to list all of the Isaiah variants in the Book of Mormon here. I have prepared an exhaustive study of these which is as yet unpublished, although it is presently circulated in manuscript form by the Foundation for Ancient Research and Mormon Studies at Brigham Young University. In my opinion, some of the very best evidence for the authenticity of the Book of Mormon as a translation from an ancient text is to be found in this study.

Subject Index

Scripture Index

NEW TESTAMENT

BOOK OF MORMON

DOCTRINE AND COVENANTS

PEARL OF GREAT PRICE